Karen Wallace lives in Herefordshire with her husband and two children. Her previous books include *Herefordshire Food* (1985).

SHROPSHIRE FOOD

KAREN WALLACE

ARCH

ISBN 0 947618 03 1

Published by
ARCH
The Hope, Kington
Herefordshire HR5 3HT

Reprinted 1990, 1993

Printed and bound in Great Britain by
Biddles Ltd, Guildford and King's Lynn

Contents

Introduction

When I started researching Shropshire Food, I had no clear picture of the county's peculiar culinary tradition. But soon a distinct personality began to emerge, a result of the county's network of market towns, cheese fairs, traditional wakes and festivals—and domestic records of the unusually large number of estates that are still intact.

Shropshire is a county of market towns. The first market was established in Bridgnorth 700 years ago, and the most recent at Hadley in Telford, in 1983. This description of Ludlow market from W. White's *All Around the Wrekin* (1860) evokes the hustle and bustle of any Saturday now.

"Rustics were crowding hither and thither, clad in fustian and broad brim, and followed by smock-frocked boys. How they grinned at the staring placards of an itinerant circus . . . while all around squadrons of ducks with legs tied . . . cocks and hens crammed into coops, all gasping with the heat, for the thermometer marked 90°.

'Moine bangs yourn,' said the red-cheeked woman to her neighbour at the next stand.

'Ah, but moine'll be sold first,' was the answer."

Food, fairs and folklore were very much bound up with each other. A village wake or fair was a special occasion and each village produced its own kind of cakes and buns for it. Many of the specialities have disappeared—notable exceptions being Shrewsbury cakes and Fig cakes, which were made in Norton. Here is an anonymous song, published in the *Market Drayton*

Advertiser in 1884, which evokes the feeling of celebration:
   "Some crying Banburys as big as the eggs of a pout,
   And gingerbread junks as big as my foot
   We ate and we ate, and we ate and we eat
   Til we could eat no more, they were so good and sweet."

There were two wakes held in the Abbey Foregate in Shrewsbury—the "cherry" wakes, where all good citizens could eat as many cherries as they could pick from the large orchard that once grew there, and the "eel-pie" wakes, when the same good citizens came to eat eels from the Severn.

Shrewsbury cakes are still as well known as Banbury buns. They were the invention of the celebrated pastry cook, Pailin, who set up trade in the city in the 18th century.

Shrewsbury itself has always been one of the principal market towns in England. Goods from all over the county were brought by carriers' cart to the market square, and stalls for butter and cheese from the rich plains of the north vied with sellers of fresh fruit and vegetables and fine local meat.

In Hinton Bank Farm in Whitchurch, the Hutchinson Smiths carry on the tradition of cheese-making and produce their own Cheshire Blue cheese, described by Nancy Eekhof-Stork in *The World Atlas of Cheese* as "One of the great 'blues' of the world".

A hundred years ago every farmer's wife in North Shropshire and Cheshire made her own cheeses, which were ripened in cool dairies before being taken to one of the great cheese markets of Whitchurch, Nantwich, Chester and Shrewsbury. Occasionally one of these cheeses would contain a delicate blue-veining; these were considered great delicacies and sent off to London. At the turn of the century, a local man, Geoffrey Hutchinson, developed this trade by deliberately selecting cheeses he thought might go blue and gradually built up the name of Cheshire Blue Cheese. However it was a hit-and-miss business, as no one really knew what caused the blue-veining. It wasn't until fifty years later that Jill and David Hutchinson Smith developed the technique of producing these special cheeses on a commercial basis.

My first task in the research for the book was to write to owners of large estates, hoping they might still have a family cookbook in the house. I received many replies and am particulary grateful

8

to Sir Michael Leighton, of Loton Park, for telling me about two cookbooks he found during a re-organisation of the library some ten years ago.

They are beautifully bound books which have been passed down through the family since the early 18th century. Most of the entries were written by Rachel Leighton at a time when, Macaulay wrote, "a Lady's Library . . . consisted of a Bible and recipe book". I have included a number of her recipes, most of which I have adapted slightly to suit modern tastes.

Another splendid source was the Radbrook Culinary Museum. This delightful relic of the Victorian era was inspired by a visit, some fifteen years ago, to the Escoffier Museum at Villeneuve-Loubet in France by members of staff from Radbrook College. A lecturer, Meg Cooper, was the driving force behind the restoration of the kitchen and there is also a scullery with a Victorian range and an earthenware sink that was part of a 17th century stable in South Shropshire.

There is a wide collection of old cookbooks and some classbooks of former students at the Catering College. I was particulary taken by the magazine *Isobel's Home Cooking*, and have taken a couple of recipes from it. It was also most interesting reading the books from the two World Wars; plum puddings to send the boys in the trenches, and the first glimmerings of an awareness of nutrition and diet.

Some of the recipes I received were very strange indeed; Mrs. Mostyn-Owen, of Woodhouse Hall in West Felton, sent me a list of local dishes that included owl soup, robin pie, leek jam, and a potato mash pudding with honey! There was one from her old gamekeeper for baby rabbits and elderflowers, a natural combination, which I adapted for chicken with excellent results.

The W.I. were tremendously helpful and I would like to thank Brenda Dryden, Joyce Mayle, and Mrs. E. Broadhurst for lending me the different editions of the W.I. cookbook. Thanks also to Meg Pybus whose book *Under the Buttercross* was a great inspiration to me

There are a number of recipes from restaurants which have been independently recommended for their excellence. Both The Old Post Office in Clun and Country Friends in Dorrington are relatively new. But in a short time, they have both built up a reputation for good food and both have received special mentions in *The Budget Good Food Guide*. I must also mention the Penny Anthony Restaurant in Ludlow, which has been established for some ten years and regularly featured in *The Good Food Guide*

I would also like to thank all the individual cooks who gave me recipes and suggestions, including Diane Davies, Carrie Eide, Stafford Whiteaker, Caroline Windsor-Clive, Pauline Napper, and Jill Hutchinson Smith. Thanks also to *The Shropshire Magazine* for its co-operation and, as usual, to Gus Woodward, of Tenbury Wells on the Shropshire/Worcestershire borders, the only true master fishmonger I know.

Special thanks must go to the staff at the Shrewsbury Records Office, who were most helpful and encouraging, and last but not least to my long-suffering husband who was fearless in his role as chief recipe-taster.

Starters

White Winter Soup

Serves 6

This creamy vegetable soup comes from a nineteenth-century household book. The addition of mint at the very end gives it a different and distinctive flavour.

> 8 oz (225 g) dried split yellow peas
> 2 pints (1.5 litres) water
> 3 parsnips, peeled and chopped
> 3 small turnips, peeled and quartered
> 2 sticks celery, chopped
> 2 leeks, white part only
> 1 oz (25 g) butter
> 4 tablespoons (4 x 15 ml spoons) single cream
> salt and cayenne pepper
> dried mint

Put the water, peas and vegetables into a saucepan. Season with salt and bring to the boil. Simmer slowly for one hour until the peas are soft. Put into a blender or rub through a sieve until smooth. Add the cream and butter (thin with milk if necessary) and blend thoroughly.

Reheat gently, check seasoning and add a few pinches of dried mint. Serve with croûtons.

Lettuce Soup

Serves 6

Pauline and John Napper live in a lovely farmhouse just outside Ludlow. John is an painter; his studio, a converted barn, is full of huge windows, with paintings and drawings hanging on every wall. They are both dedicated cooks; this is Pauline's recipe, especially handy in those inevitable summer weeks when the garden is full of lettuces.

> *about 8 oz (225 g) outside lettuce leaves, preferably cos*
> *2 tablespoons (2 x 15 ml spoons) olive oil*
> *2 cloves garlic, chopped*
> *1 medium-sized potato, peeled and chopped*
> *2 pints (about 1 litre) boiling water*
> *salt and cayenne pepper*

Heat the oil in a heavy saucepan and gently fry the garlic. When it is golden, but not brown, add the chopped lettuce leaves and the potato and stir into the oil mixture for a few minutes. Add the boiling water slowly, season with salt and cook covered for about one hour. Season and serve immediately.

Cream of Fennel Soup

Serves 6

This delicious soup comes from The Old Post Office, Clun, a delightful little restaurant which opened some two years ago. "Why Clun?" people asked. "Why not?" replied co-owners Caroline Denham and Martin Poole. In Shropshire, people will travel a long way if they know there is good food waiting for them at the other end. And since The Old Post Office gained a star rating in *The Budget Good Food Guide,* its reputation has spread across the countryside and beyond.

2 fennel bulbs, trimmed and diced (keep the trimmings)
1 oz (25 g) butter
¼ pint (150 ml) water
¼ pint (150 ml) cream

For the vegetable stock:
2 pints (about 1 litre) water
2 or 3 carrots
1 large onion
2 sticks celery
trimmings from the fennel bulbs
1 teaspoon (1 x 5 ml spoon) salt

Make the stock by simmering all the chopped stock vegetables with the water and salt in a large pan for about an hour. Strain, and keep the stock.

Melt the butter in a saucepan and simmer the fennel until soft with a little water— do not let it brown. Add the fennel mixture to the stock and put in a blender then strain.

Reheat, and just before serving, stir in the cream and heat it through.

Tomato and Haricot Soup

Serves 6

The basic recipe for this soup comes from the 1933 edition of the Shropshire W.I. cookbook.

This little green book proclaims "The Modern Home will soon be all Electric" and is full of enthusiasm for the latest gadgets like the "Easiwork Health Cooker", and a no-trouble method of preserving 600-700 eggs with just one pot of "Easiwork Egg Preservative".

8 oz (225 g) dried haricot beans, soaked
2 tablespoons (2 x 15 ml spoons) sunflower oil
1 large onion, peeled and sliced
1 clove of garlic, crushed, (optional)
1 tablespoon (1 x 15 ml spoon) tomato purée
2 medium-sized potatoes, peeled and diced
1 bay leaf
2 sprigs dried thyme
2 pints (about 1 litre) water
½ pint (300 ml) creamy milk
lemon juice
salt and pepper
chopped parsley (optional)
2 or 3 tomatoes, skinned, seeded and chopped
yoghurt to decorate (optional)

Drain the beans. Heat the oil in a heavy saucepan and put in the beans with the vegetables, garlic if used, tomato purée and herbs. Pour in boiling water and simmer, covered, for 2 or 3 hours until the beans are quite soft. Put in a blender and strain or rub through a sieve. Add the milk and season with salt, cayenne pepper and lemon juice to taste.

Reheat gently. Just before serving, stir in the chopped tomatoes and sprinkle with parsley.

Salmon Head Soup

Serves 6

While buying salmon is still an expensive proposition, a delicious and luxurious soup may be made from salmon heads. Ask your fishmonger to keep them for you.

2 salmon heads
1 pint (900 ml) fish or vegetable stock
1 pint (600 ml) béchamel sauce
1 teaspoon (1 x 5 ml spoon) tomato purée
bunch of chives
bunch of dill
scarce ¼ pint (150 ml) yoghurt
lemon juice
salt and cayenne pepper

For the béchamel sauce:
2 oz (50 g) butter
2 oz (50 g) flour
1½ pints (900 ml) milk
1 teaspoon (1 x 5 ml spoon) salt
cayenne pepper
1 medium onion, sliced

First make the béchamel sauce by melting the butter in a saucepan and mixing in the flour. Add the milk slowly to form a smooth sauce. Put in the onion and seasonings. Stir and cook gently for 15 minutes, stirring occasionally.

Meanwhile, poach the salmon heads in stock for 10 minutes. Remove with a slotted spoon and allow to cool slightly. Remove flesh, including the cheek flesh.

Return the heads to the stock and reduce it by one third by boiling rapidly. Strain. Pound the cheek flesh in a little stock, or put the whole lot into a blender with the tomato purée and the strained béchamel sauce.

Add the chopped herbs and the flaked meat and heat through gently for a few minutes. Season with lemon juice, salt and cayenne pepper. Remove from heat and stir in yoghurt to taste. Serve hot or cold.

Pigeon Soup

Serves 6 - 8

I came across many recipes for game soups in my research.

Easily the oddest came from Woodhouse Hall in West Felton, which required "one plump young barn owl, boiled for two hours."

The recipe below comes from a family cookbook belonging to the Leighton family of Loton Park, outside Shrewsbury. It is a good way of using up pigeon oddments when the succulent breasts have been removed for other dishes.

4 or more pigeon carcases
large carrot, sliced
1 large onion, sliced
2 sticks celery, chopped
bouquet garni
bunch of parsley
2 pints (about 1 litre) beef stock
port
lemon juice
salt and pepper
redcurrant jelly (optional)
croûtons

Roast the carcases in a hot oven, 400° (Gas Mark 6), for 20 minutes. Pour a little of the fat into a heavy saucepan and fry the vegetables to a golden brown. Put in the carcases; add the boiling meat stock and the bouquet garni.

Simmer gently for 2 hours with the lid on. Then strain into a clean saucepan and remove the meat from the bones. Put this in the blender with the slightly reduced stock.

Return to the pan and season with port, lemon juice, salt and pepper. If there is no port to hand, a little redcurrant jelly may be added.

Serve with freshly-made croûtons.

16

Mushrooms and Bacon with Brandy and Cream

Serves 4

This recipe comes from Charles and Pauline Whittaker who run the Country Friends restaurant in their 16th century, black and white manor house in Dorrington.
  This is one of their most popular starters.

> *8 oz (225 g) chopped bacon, smoked or green*
> *1 oz (25 g) butter*
> *1 lb (450 g) button mushrooms*
> *1 clove . garlic, crushed*
> *3 tablespoons (3 x 15 ml spoons) brandy*
> *1/2 pint (300 ml) double cream*
> *salt and pepper*
> *parmesan cheese*

Fry the bacon in butter and garlic. Add the mushrooms and toss gently. Season with salt and pepper. Add the brandy and flame it. Remove the mushrooms and bacon and keep warm. Pour the cream into the pan and boil rapidly until reduced by half.
  Return the mushrooms and bacon to the pan and boil until the sauce in thick and creamy. Turn out into hot ramekin dishes and sprinkle with parmesan cheese. Serve immediately.

Chicken Liver and Mushroom Pâté

Serves 6—8

This very simple pâté is transformed into something special by the addition of mushrooms which have been stewed in brandy, cut into chunks, and mixed in at the last moment. If you do not have brandy to hand, any red wine which has been reduced will do just as well; or use a mixture of the two.

8 oz (225 g) chicken livers
1 medium onion, diced
2 oz (50 g) butter
4 tablespoons (4 x 15 ml spoons) brandy or
2 of brandy 2 of red wine
2 teaspoons (2 x 5 ml spoons) salt
pinch cayenne pepper
5 or 6 mushrooms
3 oz (75 g) soft butter
clarified butter to cover

Melt 1 oz of butter in a saucepan and add half the brandy or red wine. Gently stew the mushrooms with the lid on, then remove to evaporate liquid. Do not allow them to dry out.

In a frying pan melt the other ounce of butter and fry the onions until they are transparent. Remove with slotted spoon to the blender, or another bowl if mixing by hand. Fry the livers in the remaining butter until they are browned on the outside but still pink and juicy on the inside. Remove to the blender or bowl. Pour the rest of the brandy or red wine into the pan with the seasoning. Stir quickly and pour on top of the livers and onions. Add the soft butter and blend until smooth. Roughly chop the mushrooms and stir into the pâté by hand.

Pour the pâté into a dish and smooth over the surface. Seal with a little clarified butter and refrigerate for at least twenty-four hours before serving.

Shrimp Pâté

Serves 6 — 8

This unusual pâté comes from Caroline Windsor-Clive who lives in a beautifully converted stable block at Oakly Park, near Ludlow. Apart from being an extremely good cook she makes superb dried flower arrangements and decorative baskets from flowers grown in her own garden.

2 lbs (almost a kilo) cooked, peeled shrimps
¼ pint (150 ml) lemon juice, or more, to taste
scarce ½ pint (300 ml) olive oil
pinch ginger
pinch paprika
salt and cayenne pepper
clarified butter to seal

Blend or pound the shrimps with the lemon juice and add the seasoning. Gradually add the olive oil. Pack into dishes and seal with clarified butter. Refrigerate for at least twenty-four hours.
   Serve with brown toast and lemon wedges.

Salmon Seviche

Serves 6

This recipe comes from the Penny Anthony restaurant in Ludlow. It is a different way to prepare salmon or salmon trout and can be eaten as a main course or as a starter on a bed of shredded lettuce garnished with cucumber. A cheaper (but no less tasty) version can be made using kipper fillets

6 pieces of salmon or salmon trout, boned and skinned

For the marinade:
½ pint (300 ml) dry white wine
1 tablespoon (1 x 15 ml spoon) sea salt
1 large onion, diced
1 clove garlic, diced
1 lemon, juice and rind
¼ pint (150 ml) sunflower oil
1 tablespoon (1 x 15 ml spoon) green peppercorns
plenty of black pepper
juice and rind of 2 oranges

Mix the marinade ingredients in a container with a lid. Put in the fish pieces, and leave covered for 1 day. Remove onto to bed of lettuce and pour a little of the marinade over as a dressing.

Cream Cheese and Herbs in a Beetroot Leaf Casing

Serves 8

This is a starter which looks good and is easy to make.

The middle layer can be varied, according to inspiration, and spinach leaves could be used instead of beetroot.

12 oz (300 g) beetroot leaves. Discard any stalks and thick-veined ones
1 lb (450 g) low fat cream cheese
8 oz (225 g) cottage cheese
good handful of fresh herbs, dill, tarragon, summer savoury, chives, basil
1 clove of garlic (optional)
1 oz (25 g) gelatine
salt
a few beetroot slices and a little yoghurt to decorate

For the tomato layer:
1 14 oz (396 g) tin tomatoes
½ onion, diced
small knob butter
1 tablespoon (1 x 15 ml spoon) lemon juice
3 teaspoons (3 x 5 ml spoons) anchovy essence
or 5 anchovy fillets, finely diced
black pepper

First make the tomato sauce. Drain the tin of tomatoes. Melt a little butter in a saucepan and gently fry the onion till soft. Put in tomatoes, lemon juice and a little pepper. Slowly reduce until the sauce is very thick and almost sticks to the bottom. Add the anchovy essence or chopped anchovies. Allow to become cold.

To wilt the beetroot leaves, put a colander over a saucepan of boiling water. Put in the leaves about five at a time for two or three minutes, until they are pliable. Oil a 9 inch round tin and line it with the wilted leaves, overlapping them to form an airtight casing. Allow some to overlap the sides for folding over later.

Finely chop the herbs or put in the blender with the cheese and the garlic and a little salt. Dissolve the gelatine in a little water over gentle heat. Pour this into the cheese as it is being mixed.

Spoon half the cheese into the leaf casing. Place two or three leaves over the top, then spread the thick tomato sauce over them. Cover this with another two or three leaves - this stops the red of the sauce leaking into the white of the cheese. Spoon in the rest of the cheese mixture.

Bring in the overlapping leaves and put on a couple more to seal in the cheese. Brush over with a little sunflower oil and cover with cling film. Refrigerate overnight.

To remove, loosen the sides with a knife and invert onto a plate. Arrange a few overlapping slices of pickled beetroot in the middle and pour a tiny sash of yoghurt over the top.

Serve with fresh bread.

Fish

Devilled Cod

Serves 6

A devilled sauce is a spicy mustard sauce, perhaps more commonly used with chicken than with fish. It was popular in the nineteenth century — the "devilled bones" of the hunt breakfast — and there are many references to it in the literature of the period. In *North and South*, Mrs Gaskell writes, "The devilled chicken tasted like sawdust."

This recipe comes from Rachel Leighton's cookbook, and bears no resemblance whatsoever to sawdust.

> *4 lb (1.8 kilos) cod*
> *½ pint (300 ml) water*
> *the fish juices*
> *½ pint (300 ml) cream*
> *1 tablespoon (1 x 15 ml spoon) prepared English mustard*
> *1 tablespoon (1 x 15 ml spoon) anchovy essence*
> *1 tablespoon (1 x 15 ml spoon) walnut or mushroom ketchup*
> *good bunch chopped fresh parsley*
> *white wine vinegar or lemon juice to taste*
> *salt and pepper*
> *tin foil*
> *butter*

Butter a piece of tin foil. Season the fish with pepper and salt and a little lemon juice and wrap up in the foil. Seal the ends carefully. Place in a large pan with the water and cook for 1 hour in a cool oven, 300°, Gas Mark 3.

When it is cooked, pour the juices into a pan and slide the fish carefully onto a hot serving dish, skin, cover and keep warm.

Make a sauce by mixing the cream with the fish juices and adding the mustard, anchovy essence and ketchup. Carefully add lemon juice or vinegar to taste. Season with salt and pepper. Boil rapidly and reduce slightly.

Pour a little of the sauce over the fish and sprinkle with chopped parsley. Serve the rest of the sauce separately.

A Most Versatile Fish Pie

Serves 6

I found this recipe in the 1954 edition of the W.I. cookbook. It came from Aileen King at Radbrook College. It is a dish which can be made with hard-boiled eggs and tomatoes for supper at home or you could add mushrooms. prawns and a couple of scallops for a dinner party.

A sauce goes well with it. For the simpler version, serve it with a plain tomato sauce, by reducing a tin of tomatoes and seasoning with salt, pepper and lemon juice.

For the special version, make a white sauce with some of the fish stock, boiled up with the prawn shells, a handful of peeled prawns, a good dash of lemon juice, or reduced white wine and a little tomato paste for colour.

> *1¼ lbs (550 g) fresh cod or haddock with trimmings*
> *3 hard-boiled eggs*
> *3 large spring onions*
> *grated lemon rind*
> *1 tin tomatoes, well drained*
> *5 tablespoons (5 x 15 ml spoons) well-seasoned thick white*

sauce made with fish stock
1 tablespoon (1 x 15 ml spoon) chopped parsley
salt and pepper
14 oz (400 g) puff pastry or 1 packet frozen
1 beaten egg
1 small onion

For the special version:
omit eggs and tomatoes and substitute:
½lb (225 g) cooked prawns with shells, saving some for the
sauce
¼lb (100 g) mushrooms, quartered
2 scallops, chopped (optional)

First make a stock from any fish bones you have managed to buy with the fish and its skin. Add the onion and season well. Simmer gently for an hour or more. Make a thick sauce using some of the fish stock, flour and butter. Season well with salt and cayenne pepper and lemon juice.

Cut the fish into small chunks and the eggs, if used, into thick rounds. Chop the spring onions. Or for the special version, peel the prawns, crush the shells and boil up with the remaining fish stock.

Roll out the pastry on a large floured board until it is quite thin. Trim the edges.

Put all the fish, onions and mushrooms (if used) into a large bowl and mix together with the thick sauce. Season well and add lemon rind and a dash of lemon juice.

Lay this mixture in the centre of the pastry and arrange the eggs and chopped tomatoes (if used) amongst the fish. Brush the edges with beaten egg and fold the pastry over, sealing all edges. Brush over with beaten egg and decorate with pastry leaves. Ease the parcel onto a wetted baking sheet and bake in the centre of a pre-heated oven 450°, Gas Mark 8, for forty-five minutes. If the top begins to burn, put a piece of foil over it.

Make the sauce of your choice (see above) and serve separately.

To Collar Salmon

Serves 6—8

To collar fish is to roll it up in a coil and cook it in a mixture of vinegar, water and spices. It was a popular way of cooking fish in the 18th and 19th centuries when refrigeration was a problem. It is a delicious way to serve cold salmon, and goes well with either a tartare sauce or a light mayonnaise flavoured with anchovies.

1 4—6 lb (about 2.5 kilos) salmon
white wine vinegar
water
salt
1 tablespoon (1 x 15 ml spoon) pickling spice with chili
1 onion, thinly sliced
good bunch marjoram and summer savoury
small piece peeled ginger
black pepper
bay leaves

Cut off the head and tail of the salmon and split him down the middle. Clean and bone the fish and lay him in a china dish. Cover with a mixture of vinegar and cold water, using two parts water to one part vinegar. Salt well. Leave this mixture for 48 hours.

Carefully remove the fish in two pieces. Pat dry and lay skin side down. Season with pepper and spinkle with the chopped herbs. Lay pieces of onion along each piece. Roll up the fish as tightly as possible, 'collar him up close' as Rachel Leighton says, and tie him with broad tape to hold in position.

Strain the marinade. Place the fish in a baking dish, and cover with the liquid, topping up with more vinegar if necessary. Add the pickling spice, the piece of bruised ginger, half a dozen peppercorns and a couple of bay leaves.

Bake in a slow oven 275°, Gas Mark 1, for 1½ - 2 hours. Allow to cool completely and serve on a bed of lettuce at least a day later. Salmon cooked this way will keep in the fridge for up to a week.

Grayling or Trout Baked with Mushrooms and Shallots

Serves 6

There is an old Shropshire saying, which is simple and direct; it goes, "Dunna swear, or thee'lt ketch no fish."

This is a good recipe, also simple and direct, for use by the families of non-swearing fishermen.

> *6 good sized fish*
> *5 shallots, chopped*
> *½ lb (225 g) mushrooms, sliced*
> *3 oz (75 g) butter*
> *almost ½ pint (150 ml) white wine*
> *almost ½ pint (150 ml) double cream*
> *big bunch of parsley*
> *lemon juice*
> *salt and pepper*

Butter an ovenproof dish large enough to hold all the fish. Sprinkle the onions, mushrooms and chopped parsley over the bottom. Season with salt and pepper. Lay the fish on the top and brush with melted butter. Bake in a hot oven, 400°, Gas Mark 6, for 10 - 15 minutes according to size, then add the wine. Baste with the juices until the flesh turns opaque, then pour over the cream and cook for another five minutes. Just before serving, squeeze a little lemon juice over the top.

Serve immediately.

Barbecued Salmon

Serves 8—10

In a magazine called *Isobel's Home Cooking*, published at the turn of the century, there was a regular feature called "Peggy's Problems". One particular problem caught my eye:

27

"Both my husband and myself are very fond of salmon. We had it for dinner last night and I boiled it very carefully so that it would be extra tasty.

When Tom saw it, his face fell visibly.

"Boiled!" he said, expressively.

"How would you have it done?" I asked.

"Anyway except boiled," the ungrateful creature remarked, and went on to tell me what lovely salmon mayonnaise he had had for lunch in the city. Well, of course after that I determined that boiled salmon should never appear on our table again.

What can you suggest?"

A moving story and a problem to which Caroline Windsor-Clive has a happy solution. Her recipe for Barbecued Salmon speaks for itself.

6—8 lb (about 3 kilos) salmon
olive oil
salt and pepper
tinfoil
½ pint (300 ml) mayonnaise mixed with fresh chopped herbs
¼ pint fromage blanc
1 barbecue with a cover

Clean and gut the salmon. Cut off the head, tail, and dorsal fin. Split down the middle and open flat. Trim off the fatty bits around the edge.

Brush a large piece of tinfoil with olive oil. Place the fish on it, skin side down, leaving 2 in all around the outside. Brush the fish with olive oil and season with salt and pepper.

Put on the grill of a barbecue, which has been lit previously, and cover. Cook until done.

Allow to cool. Mix together the mayonnaise and the fromage blanc. Serve separately.

Grayling with Watercress

Serves 6

Izaak Walton describes this fish as one who "lurks close all winter, but is very pleasant and jolly after mid-April . . . the flower of fishes".

He is a first cousin of the trout, and his preference for unpolluted rivers like the Teme is reflected in the delicate flavour of his flesh.

The best way to eat grayling is the simplest; fried in butter and lemon and served on a bed of watercress, another native of clean Shropshire rivers.

6 grayling, cleaned, gutted and scaled
12 oz (300 g) butter
seasoned flour
lemon quarters
2 good bunches watercress
salt, pepper, lemon juice

Clarify half the butter. Coat the fish in the flour and shake off the surplus. Spread the watercress in a large serving dish, discarding the stalks.

Heat the clarified butter in a large frying pan and fry the fish until golden brown. Turn once only. Lay the fish on top of the watercress and keep warm. Wipe off the pan and melt the rest of the butter. When it is foaming, add a little lemon juice and swirl together. Pour this mixture over the fish and serve immediately with lemon quarters.

Trout stuffed with fresh herbs and butter, and baked en papillote

Serves 6

This recipe, from The Old Post Office, brings out the trout's delicate flavour and keeps the fish moist. Use only fresh herbs, as dried ones are too strong. Allow one fish per person.

> 6 8 oz (225 g) fish, wiped and gutted
> For each fish, the stuffing is:
> ½ oz (15 g) soft butter
> ¼ clove garlic, crushed
> 1 teaspoon (1 x 5 ml spoon) chopped fresh rosemary
> 1 teaspoon (1 x 5 ml spoon) chopped fresh parsley
> sunflower or olive oil
> tin foil
> sprig of rosemary and marjoram, lemon slice to garnish

Mix all the stuffing ingredients together and stuff the fish. Lightly brush the fish all over with the oil, especially the tail, to stop it from sticking. Carefully arrange a slice of lemon and sprigs of rosemary and marjoram on one side of the trout to decorate.

Place each trout on a piece of tin foil and wrap it up, not too tightly, in a parcel. This is the "papillote". The fish bakes in its own steam and remains beautifully succulent.

Place the trout on a baking tray and bake in a fairly hot oven, 425°, Gas Mark 7, for 20 - 25 minutes. The cooking time will vary according to the size of the fish.

To serve, unwrap the trout and carefully lift off the tinfoil onto a warmed plate.

A Dainty Lunch with Cod

Serves 6

I found this recipe at the Radbrook Culinary Museum in a magazine series called *Isobel's Home Cooking* published in 1898. I shall give you part of the original introduction which speaks for itself.

"A dainty lunch and how to serve it.

The word 'lunch' is derived from the Welsh 'llwne', which is a variation of 'lump'. In bygone days lunch or luncheon meant simply a lump of bread and cheese taken between meals; but now lunch, more especially among the upper classes, has become a fashionable meal . . . and many ladies who give lunch parties even take a pride in preparing the salad themselves."

I have adapted the recipe slightly to include more fresh vegetables and have put it on a bed of shredded lettuce, to save ladies in the 1980's from having to prepare the salad themselves!

> *2 lbs (almost 1 kilo) filleted cod*
> *butter*
> *1 lb (450 g) mixed fresh vegetables, peas, snap peas, courgettes (cut into sticks), red pepper, green beans*
> *good bunch of fresh herbs, dill, basil, tarragon etc.*
> *3/4 pint (450 ml) dry white wine or half of water*
> *2 large egg yolks*
> *3 tablespoons (3 x 15 ml spoons) thick cream*
> *4 oz (125 g) butter*
> *lemon juice*
> *salt and cayenne pepper*
> *chives and chervil to decorate*
> *1 crisp lettuce, shredded*

Melt a little butter in a heavy, shallow pan and gently fry the prepared vegetables. Break the cod fillets into chunks and add these to the vegetables, then pour over the wine and the fresh chopped herbs. Bring to the boil and simmer for five minutes.

Lift the fish and vegetables out with a slotted spoon, drain well, cover and set aside.

Add the cream to the fish stock and reduce by half. Strain this liquid and allow to cool slightly. Beat the yolks into the warm liquid and stir over a very low heat until the sauce begins to thicken. Then lift the pan from the heat and add the butter, a little bit at a time, stirring constantly.

Season the sauce with salt and pepper and a little lemon juice and allow to cool down.

Arrange the shredded lettuce on a large serving plate and season with salt and pepper and a little lemon juice.

Drain off any liquid from the fish and vegetables and put on the lettuce. Stir the cool sauce and pour over the top. Sprinkle with chopped chives and chervil and serve.

Poultry and Game

Pigeon Stewed with Cabbage

Serves 6

This is a version of a traditional recipe from in Rachel Leighton's cookbook. The pigeon would originally have come from dovecotes. According to Meg Pybus in her splendid book *Under the Buttercross* only the landed gentry and the church were allowed to keep pigeons in proper dovecotes because of crop damage. In spite of this, many a farmhouse had its own box on the side of the barns.

Some pigeons had more important duties and never finished up on the kitchen table; the loft at Styche Hall kept military pigeons, which remained in active service for the duration of the last war.

A woodpigeon has a pleasant gamey flavour and is an ideal candidate for terrines and game pies. A specially bred domestic pigeon has less flavour, but the meat is more tender and it takes less time to cook than its wild cousin.

In the original recipe the cabbage was overcooked. This version leaves it still slightly crisp but succulent with the absorbed pigeon juices.

6 pigeons
2 tablespoons (2 x 15 ml spoons) butter
12 oz (325 g) streaky bacon, smoked or green
1 lb (450 g) pickling onions
dry white wine
beef stock (about ½ pint (300 ml) each)
1 teaspoon (1 x 5 ml spoon) dried thyme
salt and pepper
2 medium sized Savoy cabbages
lemon juice

Cut the bacon into small pieces and fry gently in the melted butter. Put in the pigeons and brown all over, then add the onions and cook until they are a golden brown. Take out the pigeons and lay, breast side down, in a heavy casserole. Pour off any surplus fat and pour in the white wine and beef stock. Bring this mixture to the boil, scraping well to collect any leftovers. Pour over the pigeons so they are just covered. Lay a piece of foil or a couple of butter papers over the top and cover. Simmer gently for an hour or more.

Meanwhile, trim the outer leaves from the cabbages and make two cuts across their bases. Put them both into a saucepan of boiling salted water and cook for 5—8 minutes. Drain carefully and open up the centre leaves into a nest for the pigeons.

Remove the pigeons from the casserole and put three in each cabbage.Then put the whole lot back into the casserole and bake for a further half hour at 350°, Gas Mark 4.

When everything is ready, arrange it on a hot plate and keep warm. Skim off as much fat as possible and reduce the sauce to concentrate the flavour. Season and add a dash of lemon juice if desired. Pour over the pigeons and serve with new carrots and potatoes.

Chicken with Cucumber

Serves 6

Cooking meat with cucumber was popular in the 18th century. I found recipes for lamb and rabbit and adapted this one for chicken. A rather lazy version, I suppose, in that it can all be cooked in the one frying pan but a delicious summer recipe when cucumbers are plentiful and there is fresh mint in the garden.

1 jointed chicken
2 large cucumbers
4 tablespoons (4 x 15 ml spoons) white wine or lemon juice
oil
seasoned flour
1 pint (600 ml) chicken stock
6 fl oz (175 ml) double cream
salt and cayenne pepper
bunch chopped fresh mint

Peel the cucumbers and chop into short, fat sticks. Blanch in boiling, salted water and drain thoroughly. Pat dry.

Coat the chicken in the seasoned flour. Heat the oil in a heavy frying pan and fry the chicken to a golden brown. Be careful not to burn it. Add the white wine and cook until it has reduced to almost nothing. Stir in the cucumber sticks and add enough stock to almost cover the chicken pieces. Simmer gently with the top off until just cooked.

Turn up the heat and add the cream. Stir gently until the sauce thickens. Check the seasoning and just before serving sprinkle with chopped mint.

Chicken in Puff Pastry

Serves 6

This delicious recipe comes from the Whittakers' Country Friends Restaurant in Dorrington. Charles Whittaker's reputation as a pastry chef is spreading far and wide, and this mouth-watering mixture of cream cheese and chicken encased in puff pastry is his own concoction.

The parcels could be made in advance and kept in a refrigerator. At any rate, they should be slightly chilled before putting into a hot oven — a secret of successful puff pastry.

> *6 chicken breasts, skinned and boned*
> *puff pastry*
> *1 lb (450 g) cream cheese*
> *5 oz (125 g) melted butter*
> *2 tablespoons (2 x 15 ml spoons) chopped fresh herbs*
> *large clove garlic*
> *salt*
> *1 egg, beaten*

Beat the cream cheese until smooth and light, add the garlic and herbs and season with salt. Slowly add the melted butter.

With a sharp knife, make a deep incision into the chicken breasts and stuff with the cream cheese mixture. Roll out the puff pastry and cut into squares big enough to wrap up the chicken. Fold over the edges and pinch together.

Chill. Preheat oven to 450°, Gas Mark 8. Paint the pastry parcels with beaten egg and place in the middle of the oven. Cook until brown, about 8 minutes. Cut in half and serve immediately.

Chicken with Elderflower and Baby Turnips

Serves 6

This is a recipe I adapted from an eighteenth century Ellesmere Elderflower and Baby Rabbit pie, a dish kept for celebrations only. It is essential to marinate the chicken for at least two days and to use only small, juicy turnips.

> *1 chicken, jointed*
> *1 pint (600 ml) elderflower wine or*
> *2/3 water to 1/3 lemon juice and 3 fresh elderflowers*
> *sunflower oil*
> *2 oz (50 g) butter*
> *1 lb (450 g) baby turnips, washed and trimmed*
> *lemon thyme*
> *salt and cayenne pepper*
> *2 tablespoons (2 x 15 ml spoons) flour*
> *glass white wine (optional)*
> *handful chopped parsley*

Prick the chicken pieces all over with a sharp fork. Place in a bowl and pour over the elderflower wine or the lemon juice and water with the elderflowers, or for a sronger taste, both together. Leave for two days, turning from time to time.

Heat a little oil in a heavy casserole dish. Remove the chicken from its marinade and pat dry Brown them in the oil and set aside. Pour out the oil and wipe over the dish. Melt half the butter and gently cook the turnips for a couple of minutes. Put back the chicken pieces and add the thyme.

Strain the marinade and bring to the boil. Pour over the chicken. Cover with foil or butter papers and a lid. Cook in a moderate oven 325°, Gas Mark 3, for 45 minutes.

Remove the chicken and turnips with a slotted spoon and keep warm. Strain the cooking liquid into a saucepan and reduce slightly. Melt butter in the casserole dish and work in the flour. Slowly add the strained stock, and a little wine if desired, and cook until smooth and thick. Season with salt and pepper and pour over the chicken and turnips. Sprinkle with parsley and serve immediately.

If you prefer a whole chicken, follow the same method, adding a little extra cooking time. At the last moment, pour a little sauce over the bird, sprinkle with parsley and serve the rest of the sauce separately.

Pot Roasted Pheasant

Serves 4

Pheasants are in season from October to February. They are one of the most delicious of the game birds, as long as they are hung properly. Traditionally, a bird was not ready to be cooked until the blood began to drop from the bill. Anything from two to three weeks in cold, frosty weather and less than a week in warmer. damp weather should allow the flesh to acquire its distinctive flavour.

This recipe comes from Marielle at the Restaurant in St. Mary's Street, Market Drayton and first appeared in *Under The Buttercross* by Meg Pybus.

> *1 pheasant weighing about 2½ lbs (1.5 kg)*
> *2 thin slices streaky bacon*
> *15 small pickling onions*
> *15 button mushrooms*
> *4 fl ozs (150 ml) brandy*
> *5 oz (125 g) butter*
> *Thyme*
> *Bay leaf*
> *Oil*
> *Salt and Pepper*

Season the bird inside and out with freshly ground black pepper and salt. Melt a knob of butter with one tablespoon of oil. Without burning the butter, brown the pheasant on all sides. Pour over a little of the brandy and set alight, turning the pheasant over in the liquid.

Remove the pheasant and lard with the bacon. Put it breast side down, in a heavy casserole with seasoned onions and mushrooms, the rest of the butter and brandy, a sprig of thyme, a bay leaf and a small glass of water. Cover and put in a preheated oven, 425°, Gas Mark 7, for 20 minutes. Then turn the bird on its back and cook uncovered for a final five minutes until golden brown.

If the sauce is still too liquid, take out the pheasant and keep it warm, then reduce the stock to the required consistency.

Rabbit Smothered with Onions

Serves 6

Onions seem to play a large part in old Shropshire remedies. Onion poultices were used to draw out inflammation and raw onions were peeled and left in rooms to collect bacteria and prevent the spread of disease.

Until some 25 years ago and the advent of myxomatosis, rabbit provided the only regular source of fresh meat for many families. Since that time, although rabbit numbers have to some extent recovered, rabbit has gone out of fashion as fast foods and frozen dishes have taken over the popular market.

Today, a good butcher will keep rabbit, which is not expensive, and a meatier alternative to chicken.

This recipe therefore combines frugality with good health, and is a delicious introduction to eating rabbit.

> *1 young rabbit, jointed*
> *dry cider and water to cover*
> *bouquet garni*
> *salt and pepper*
> *3 lbs (1.8 kg) onions, peeled and left whole*
> *5 oz (125 g) butter*
> *1 tablespoon (1 x 15 ml spoon) flour*
> *¼ pint (150 ml) cream*
> *nutmeg (optional)*

Put the rabbit pieces and the onions in a heavy casserole. Cover with a mixture of cold water and cider, add the bouquet garni and season well with pepper and salt. Bring to the boil and simmer until cooked.

Remove the onions with a slotted spoon and chop them up. Put them in a clean saucepan. Mix in the butter and cook until the onions are golden. Then mix in the flour and cook for a couple more minutes. Stir in the cream and check the seasoning, adding a little nutmeg if you like it.

Take out the rabbit pieces and arrange them on a hot serving dish. Pour the onions over the top and serve immediately.

The leftover stock should be kept and used for making soup.

A 'Frigazee' of Rabbit

Serves 6

I found this basic recipe in Rachel Leighton's cookbook, and have adapted it slightly with the aid of some spring onions and smoked bacon. It keeps well and, like most stews, should be made a day in advance, to improve the flavour.

1 young rabbit, jointed
20 round spring onions
5 oz (125 g) mushrooms
3 rashers smoked bacon
good bunch fresh herbs
1½ oz (40 g) flour
1 tablespoon (1 x 15 ml spoon) oil
1 oz (25 g) butter
lemon juice
salt and pepper

For the stock:
1 carcase
1 carrot
1 onion
1 stick celery
bouquet garni (optional)
salt and pepper
oil

First make the stock, preferably the day before. In a heavy saucepan, heat a little oil and brown the carcase lightly. Add the onion, carrot, celery and herbs and cover with water. Season well and simmer for an hour or so. Strain and set aside. Better still, when it has cooled, chill slightly and skim off any fat that surfaces.

In a heavy casserole dish, heat the oil and the butter and gently fry the chopped bacon. Add the rabbit pieces and lightly brown. Then add the onions and mushrooms. Cook for a couple of minutes, then mix in the chopped herbs and the flour. Stir well and add a good dash of lemon juice, then the boiling stock to cover. Season well and cover with a butter paper or a piece of foil. Put the lid on and cook in a moderate oven, 325°, Gas Mark 4, for 1½ hours.

Venison in a Blackcurrant Sauce

Serves 8

This recipe comes from Charles Whittaker at the Country Friends Restaurant in Dorrington. He writes, "During the winter months venison features greatly on our menus. This is a dish well worth all the preparation."

This recipe uses a boned saddle of venison, with the "eye" removed and the trimmings kept for making stock. If you want a slightly more gamey flavour, marinate the venison in a mixture of red wine, sliced onion, a good oil, salt and pepper for at least twenty four hours.

8 lb (about 3.5 kg) boned saddle of venison
8 tablespoons (8 x 15 ml spoons) blackcurrants, soaked in
red wine vinegar for at least two weeks
¼ pint (150 ml) double cream
8 oval-shaped slices of bread, soaked in melted butter
blackcurrant jam
chopped parsley
venison stock (see recipe)
salt and pepper
butter

Cut the eye of the saddle in one long piece from each side. Trim
all the sinew off. The prepared meat should look like a filet of
beef. Cut each strip into four pieces.

Brown the remaining meat trimmings and bones along with
some onion, carrot and celery. Season and cover with water.
Bring to the boil and simmer for four hours. Strain, reduce by a
quarter, cool and skim.

Lightly brown the soaked bread in the oven. Spread with
blackcurrant jam and sprinkle with chopped parsley. Fry the
venison in a little butter to seal, lightly cover with butter paper or
buttered foil to avoid any drying out and cook in a moderate oven
350°, Gas Mark 4, for 10 minutes or so. Venison should be eaten
slightly rare.

Meanwhile, put the stock in a saucepan and reduce by half.
Add the blackcurrants and then the cream and reduce further.
Thicken with a good knob of butter and check seasoning.

Put the venison on the prepared slices of bread pour the sauce
over the top. Serve immediately.

Meat

A Hodge-Podge of Lamb

Serves 6

I found this recipe in a battered little book at the Shrewsbury Records office. It is very versatile and could be made with any combination of vegetables or any number of chops. Its goodness lies in the fact that no water is added and the meat cooks in its own juices and those of the vegetables.

> *6 large middle cut lamb chops*
> *2 onions, peeled and sliced*
> *1 oz (25 g) butter*
> *a little oil*
> *1 lb (450 g) spinach, washed, dried and roughly chopped*
> *3 good courgettes, thickly sliced*
> *good handful of chopped fresh herbs*
> *lemon juice*
> *salt and pepper*

Melt a little of the butter and the oil in a heavy pan. Lightly brown the chops to seal and set aside. Fry the onions and add the chopped herbs. Stir in the spinach, until it melts down. Season with salt and pepper. Put the chops on top of the spinach. Arrange the sliced courgettes over the top. Dot with butter and sprinkle a little lemon juice over the top. Season with salt and pepper. Cover with a piece of foil.

Cook with the lid on in a moderate oven, 325°, Gas Mark 4, for 1 1/4 hours.

Lo Brasucadou

Serves 4

This recipe comes from Pauline Napper who lives near Ludlow now but has travelled extensively with her husband John, who is a painter. Pauline has always been interested in food and this recipe is both unusual and economical. It is, however, most important to use only the youngest, best quality lamb. Frozen New Zealand lamb will not do!

> *1 breast of young lamb*
> *2 cloves garlic, crushed*
> *10 freshly bruised black peppercorns*
> *1 teaspoon (1 x 5 ml spoon) ground coriander or*
> *1 teaspoon (1 x 5 ml spoon) ground cumin*
> *juice of a lemon*

Prick the breast of lamb all over with a sharp knife. Make a paste from the garlic, peppercorns, coriander or cumin and the lemon juice. Rub this well into the meat and spread any that is left over into the fat side and leave for at least 4 hours.

Roast in a hot oven, 400°, Gas Mark 6, for about forty minutes. Serve with a purée of green lentils and a green salad.

Ragout of Lambs' kidneys and mushrooms

Serves 6

This recipe comes from the Old Post Office at Clun. It is definitely for kidney lovers. The secret is to use only fresh kidneys and not to cook them for too long, then they stay succulent rather than drying up into little hard lumps. Homemade stock rather than the ever ready cube makes all the difference as well.

> *12 lambs' kidneys*
> *Olive oil*
> *1 dessertspoon (1 x 10 ml spoon) plain wholemeal flour*
> *salt and black pepper*
> *½ pint (300 ml) red wine or brown stock (or a mixture of both)*
> *½ lb (225 g) mushrooms, sliced*

Two or three hours before cooking, trim and slice the kidneys, place them in a flat, shallow dish and smother in freshly grated black pepper. Cover and leave in the fridge until you are ready to cook them.

Heat the oil in a large frying pan. Gently seal the kidneys on both sides. Remove from the pan and set aside. Make a sauce, stir in the flour, then beat in the stock or red wine. Bring to the boil and simmer for five minutes. Add the mushrooms and cook gently for two minutes. Add the kidneys and simmer for no more than five minutes, until the kidneys are just done. Season to taste, but beware of oversalting.

Serve with fresh spinach and new or mashed potatoes.

Shropshire Spring Lamb Chops with Damson Sauce

Serves 6

This recipe first appeared in *The Shropshire Magazine*. It makes a delicious change from mint sauce and the slightly tart flavour of the damson complements the sweet taste of fresh young lamb. It is also a good way of using surplus damsons you may have enthusiastically frozen the year before.

> *12 best end of neck chops*
> *1 lb (450 g) damsons*
> *½ pint (300 ml) dry white wine*
> *good bunch chopped fresh herbs*
> *salt and pepper*
> *sugar*
> *butter*

First make a purée by boiling the damsons with a tiny bit of water and enough sugar to just remove the acidity from the taste. Cook until soft and rub through a sieve. Set aside.

Season the chops with salt and pepper, dot with butter and sprinkle with chopped herbs. Grill to taste. Set aside and keep warm. Drain the meat juices into a saucepan and add the white wine. Boil rapidly to reduce by half and stir in the damson purée.

Serve the chops on hot plates with a good dollop of damson purée on each.

Fruity Roast Pork

Serves 6

Pork goes well with both fruit and vegetables. This dish is a mixture of many recipes I have looked at and is a refreshing change for a Sunday lunch. A little cider added to the gravy makes all the difference.

> *1 shoulder, loin or leg of pork on the bone*
> *6 large Bramley apples*
>
> *2 tablespoons (2 x 15 ml spoons) brown sugar*
> *3 oz (75 g) dried apricots*
> *2 oz (50 g) chopped walnuts*
> *4 tablespoons (4 x 15 ml spoons) toasted brown breadcrumbs*
> *1 clove garlic (optional)*
> *1 small orange*
> *a good pinch ground ginger*
> *1 teaspoon (1 x 5 ml spoon) cinnamon*
> *dash angostura bitters (optional)*
> *2 tablespoons (2 x 15 ml spoons) melted butter*
> *salt and pepper*
> *oil*
> *cider*

Score the rind all over with a very sharp knife and season well with salt. Leave for at least twelve hours, if possible.

Finely chop the garlic and apricots and mix with the walnuts, breadcrumbs, spices, melted butter, the juice of the orange and the grated rind. Season well.

Put to one side enough of the stuffing to fill each apple and mix with the brown sugar. Carefully core the apples and stuff them.

Take the meat and make deep cuts with a sharp knife, fill these and any other gaps with the rest of the stuffing. Rub the joint all over with a little oil and sprinkle with a little more salt. Put into a hot oven, 425°, Gas Mark 7, for about 25 minutes, until the crackling starts to brown then turn down to 325°, Mark 3 and cook for a further 1½ - 2 hours depending on the size of the joint. (Allow roughly 35 minutes to the lb.) About an hour before the end of cooking time, pour a little cider into the roasting pan and put in your stuffed apples.

When the meat is cooked, remove it carefully to a hot serving dish and arrange the apples around it. Make the gravy with the juices in the pan and a little cider. Allow to boil for a couple of minutes to reduce slightly. Serve separately.

Shrewsbury Stew with Mustard and Herb Dumplings

Serves 6

This recipe comes from the classbook of a student attending Radbrook Catering College in 1917. During that period, the lessons were divided into two sections, wartime and peacetime cookery.

Each student was asked to list the attributes of each dish and this particular one scored highly. Cheaper cuts of meat, little fuel, and few pans are used and all the ingredients are cooked together to maximize nourishment. It is certainly filling and I find dumplings are always popular with children.

2 lbs (almost 1 kg) shin beef, cubed and coated with seasoned flour
2 tablespoons (2 x 15 ml spoons) plain flour
1½ oz (40 g) dripping or butter or a little oil
1 pint (600 ml) strong beef stock
1 swede, peeled and cubed
2 onions, peeled and quartered
2 carrots, peeled and chopped
1 turnip, peeled and chopped
dash Worcestershire sauce
2 tablespoons (2 x 15 ml spoons) tomato ketchup
salt and pepper

For the dumplings:
4 oz (100 g) self-raising flour (or plain with baking powder)
2 oz (50 g) shredded suet
good pinch dried mustard
good pinch dried mixed herbs.
1 teaspoon (1 x 5 ml spoon) minced onion
chopped parsley (optional)
salt and pepper

Melt the fat in a heavy casserole dish and when it is quite hot, brown the meat on all sides. Remove with a slotted spoon and add the vegetables. When they have browned for a few minutes return the meat to the pot. Stir in the flour and add the ketchup and worcestershire sauce. Pour in the boiling beef stock and season well.

Cook, covered, in a warm oven 300°, Gas Mark 3, for 2 hours. Make the dumplings by sifting together the flour, salt and mustard, then add the suet, herbs and onion. Mix to a stiff dough with a little water and shape into small balls.

Take casserole out of the oven and drop in the dumplings. Cook for another 30 minutes. Check seasoning and serve.

Mock Game

Serves 6

These little parcels may be the Shropshire equivalent of Herefordshire's Beef Olives. They are a little fiddly to make but well worth the effort as they taste delicious. Serve surrounded by the gravy and garnished with croutes of fried bread.

2 lbs (almost 1 kg) steak
bacon rashers
1 oz (25 g) dripping or butter
1 large onion, finely chopped
1 heaped tablespoon (1 x 15 ml spoon) capers
1 teaspoon (1 x 5 ml spoon) grated lemon rind
1 glass port
1 dessertspoon (1 x 10 ml spoon) red wine vinegar
2 dessertspoons (2 x 10 ml spoons) red currant jelly
good beef stock
plain flour
cornflour
salt and pepper
6 or more slices fried bread

Remove the rinds from the bacon and cut the steak into strips. Lay a piece of bacon on each strip of meat, dredge with seasoned flour and roll up with the bacon on the inside. Tie each one with cotton and fry in the dripping. Add the onion and capers and fry gently. Then add the lemon rind, vinegar, red currant jelly and just enough boiling stock to cover. Cover and cook in a moderate oven 300°, Gas Mark 3, until tender.

Remove the meat parcels, add the port and reduce the liquid by one third. Thicken the sauce with cornflour and cook a little longer. Season to taste and add a few more capers if you like.

Remove cotton from the meat and arrange on a hot serving dish. Pour the gravy over the top and serve garnished with croutes of fried bread.

Beefsteak stewed with Pickled Walnuts and Mushrooms

Serves 6

Judging from Rachel Leighton's cookbook, recipes for pickling walnuts have changed little over the years. They are easy to do and quite delicious with cheese and salads, so it is well worth tracking down a mature walnut tree and a willing owner.

In this recipe pickled walnuts are used in place of oysters (even rarer than mature walnut trees) to add a piquant and unusual flavour to a rich beef stew.

> *2 lbs (almost 1 kg) shin beef, cubed and coated in seasoned flour*
> *10 - 12 pickled walnuts*
> *½ lb (225 g) mushrooms, preferably field mushrooms*
> *2 oz (50 g) butter*
> *1 tablespoon (1 x 15 ml spoon) dark brown sugar*
> *2 tablespoons (2 x 15 ml spoons) red wine vinegar*
> *beef stock or water*
> *2 oz (50 g) port or red wine*
> *2 tablespoons (2 x 15 ml spoons) butter*
> *2 tablespoons (2 x 15 ml spoons) flour*
> *salt and pepper*

Melt the butter in a heavy casserole dish and brown the meat on all sides until it is a good dark colour. Add the sugar and the vinegar and pour in enough boiling stock to just cover the meat. Cover and cook in a warm oven, 300°, Gas Mark 3 for 2 hours. Then add the mushrooms and the pickled walnuts and cook for a further 20 minutes.

When it is all ready, add the port and mash the flour and butter together. Roll it into little knobs and add them to the gravy which should be kept just below boiling. Check the seasoning and serve.

Sour Plum Pot Roast

Serves 6

I like the combination of meat and fruit and this recipe can be made with a fresh joint of meat or one taken straight from the freezer. I use a frozen one because the meat stays more moist and is easier to cut into slices.

> 4 lb (1.8 kg) brisket or chuck roast
> 1 tablespoon (1 x 15 ml spoon) oil
> 3 dessertspoons (3 x 10 ml spoons) plum chutney
> 1 tablespoon (1 x 15 ml spoon) tomato paste
> 1 tablespoon (1 x 15 ml spoon) lemon juice
> 1 tablespoon (1 x 15 ml spoon) walnut ketchup or Worcestershire   sauce
> 1 teaspoon (1 x 5 ml spoon) dried mustard
> ½ pint (30 ml) boiling water
> salt and pepper

Heat the oil in a heavy casserole dish and brown the meat on all sides. Remove and put to on side. Put all the other ingredients in except the water and mix to a small paste. Put the meat back in and smear the paste all over the meat. Add the water. Cover the meat with a piece of foil and put the lid on.

Cook in a slow oven, 275°–300°, Gas Mark 2–3, for 2½ hours if fresh and 3½ if frozen.

Take out the meat and keep warm on a serving dish. Boil the sauce until it is thick. Check seasoning, cut the meat into good slices and serve the sauce separately.

Light Lunches and Suppers

Fidget, Fitchett or Shropshire Pie

Serves 8

I have tried to track down the origins of this pie with a marked lack of success. 'Fitchet' is a 17th century word for a weasel or polecat but I can't believe that it was an ingredient in the first Shropshire pie!

The pie itself is a mouth-watering combination of apples, onions and bacon. The filling can also used for a raised pie by using half and half bacon and minced pork and half the amount of stock.

This particular recipe comes from the café at Acton Scott Working Farm Museum, whose food is recommended in *The Budget Good Food Guide*. The museum demonstrates life as it would have been on an upland farm from about 1875 to 1920, that is before the introduction of the petrol engine. Men work with Shire horses demonstrating nineteenth century farming techniques and the stock includes breeds of cows, sheep, pigs and poultry rarely seen to-day.

1 lb (450 g) shortcrust pastry
2 lbs (900 g) unsmoked minced bacon
8 oz (225 g) onions, chopped
1 lb (450 g) cooking apples, peeled and sliced
½ pint (300 ml) strong chicken stock
a little sugar
mixed herbs
salt and pepper

Place the minced bacon in the bottom of a deep pie dish. Put the apples and onions in layers over the top and season each layer with the herbs, sugar, salt and pepper. Pour the strong chicken stock over the whole thing.

Bake in an oven preheated to 325°, Gas Mark 4, for 30 minutes. Roll out a pastry lid and put it on top of the mixture. Bake for a further 20 minutes at 375°, Gas Mark 6.

A Raised Pork Pie with Onions and Herbs

Serves 8

The traditional pork pie is seasoned with spices like cinnamon, nutmeg and allspice. This version uses fresh herbs, onion, garlic and hard boiled eggs and is perfect for lunch or a salad supper. Keep it for at least a day before eating so the flavours have time to mingle.

2 lbs (900 g) boned pork with a 1:4 fat to meat ratio
½ lb (225 g) streaky bacon
1 medium onion, diced
1 - 2 cloves garlic, crushed
a good handful fresh herbs,chopped
2 teaspoons anchovy essence

4 hard boiled eggs
salt and pepper
lemon juice

For the hot water crust:
7 fl oz (200 ml) water
6 oz (150 g) lard
1 lb (450 g) plain flour
1 teaspoon (1 x 5 ml spoon) salt
1 beaten egg
1 dessertspoon (1 x 10 ml spoon) icing sugar

Save the best bits of pork and cut them into small pieces. Mince the rest of the meat together and mix by hand with all the other ingredients, including the diced pieces, in a large bowl. Cover and leave for twenty four hours.

Make the pastry by putting the water and lard in a large saucepan and bringing them to the boil. Turn the heat off and tip all the flour, sugar and salt into the saucepan and stir it in quickly until it forms a ball. When the dough can be handled easily, take off a quarter or so for a lid and put the rest into your tin and spread it with your fingers over the bottom and ease it up the side. Make sure there are no cracks. This is not difficult as long as the pastry is not too hot or too cold.

Put half the meat mixture into tin and press down the hard-boiled eggs. Cover with the rest of the meat. Roll out the remaining pastry to form a lid and seal it with beaten egg. Make a central hole in the lid and keep it open with a curled piece of cardboard or something similar. Decorate the pie with pastry leaves if desired and paint the whole with beaten egg.

Put the pie in an oven preheated to 400°, Gas Mark 6, and cook for half an hour, to brown the pastry. Then lower the heat to 325°, Gas Mark 3 and bake for a further two hours. When cooked, ease around the edge with a sharp knife and allow to cool completely. Leave for at least a day before eating.

Cheshire Blue Savouries

Makes about 20 balls

Blue cheese has always been a mystery; for many years no-one knew what freak conditions created the delicate blue veining that runs through one cheese while its neighbour is covered in mould.

Cheesemakers were convinced that a hard-pressed blue cheese could not be made successfully on a commercial basis; however, the Hutchinson-Smith family decided that where there was a will there was a way, and now this unique cheese is made by them at their farm in Whitchurch and distributed all over the country and abroad.

Hutchinson's Blue has won many prizes at the famous Nantwich Cheese Show and is now internationally acclaimed.

Such a fine cheese should be eaten on its own; however, this recipe, discovered in the Shrewsbury Records Office, is a good way of using up leftovers.

½ pint (300 ml) water
2 oz (50 g) butter
3 oz (75 g) flour
2 oz (50 g) breadcrumbs
3 oz (75 g) grated Blue Cheese
2 oz (50 g) Blue Cheese cut into small cubes
2 eggs
salt and cayenne pepper
sunflower oil

Put the water and butter into a saucepan and boil until the butter melts. Stir in the flour and cook for a couple of minutes. The mixture will form a soft ball and come away from the sides of the pan.

Remove from the heat and beat in the two eggs. Season well and stir in the breadcrumbs. Allow to cool completely.

Form into small balls with floured hands and press a lump of cheese into the middle of each.

Deep fry until golden brown. Put balls on absorbent paper to soak up any excess oil. Serve with mustard and a fresh green salad.

Chicken Rolls stuffed with Blue Cheese and Bacon

Serves 6

This recipe comes from Jill Hutchinson Smith. The combination of the cheese and the chicken is extremely good and a delicious surprise to anyone who has not tasted the cheese before.

> *4 oz (100 g) Blue Cheshire Cheese*
> *6 chicken breasts, flattened with a mallet*
> *8 oz (225 g) smoked streaky bacon*
> *3 oz (75 g) butter*
> *chicken stock*
> *white wine*
> *arrowroot*
> *salt and pepper*
> *chicory leaves*
> *salt and pepper*
> *oil*
> *button thread or toothpicks*

Pound the butter and cheese together to make a smooth paste. Spread out the chicken breasts and season with salt and pepper. Smear the chicken with the cheese mixture and roll up as tightly as possible. Cut into short lengths.

Wrap a little bacon around each roll and secure with a toothpick or tie with thread. Heat some oil in a heavy frying pan.

If you are planning to eat them cold, fry gently until they are cooked. Place on greaseproof paper and allow to cool. Cover until needed.

For a hot supper, brown the rolls lightly. Put them in a casserole dish and just cover with chicken stock. Simmer gently until they are tender, about 40 minutes.

Remove the rolls with a slotted spoon. Take out the toothpicks and arrange on a serving dish on a fan of chicory leaves. Reduce the stock by half and add a little wine. Check the seasoning. For a thicker sauce mix in a little arrowroot. Pour the sauce over the chicken and serve immediately.

Fresh Vegetable Pancakes with Hazelnut Sauce

Serves 6

Penny Anthony's Restaurant was the first 'bistro' to open in Ludlow. Penny runs the restaurant along the lines of those in the French provinces. There is a fixed-price menu and the emphasis is on good, honest food for good, honest prices.

These pancakes can be made with any seasonal vegetables such as beans, broccoli, beansprouts, spinach, courgettes etc. They are simple to do while the hazlenut sauce makes them different and delicious.

Pancake batter made from:
8 oz (225 g) plain flour
2 eggs
¾ pint (450 ml) milk
¼ pint (150 ml) water
1 teaspoon (1 x 5 ml spoon) salt

2 lbs (about a kilo) fresh vegetables
fresh ginger, peeled and finely diced
good bunch chopped fresh herbs
salt and pepper

For the béchamel sauce:
2 oz (50 g) butter
2 oz (50 g) flour
1¼ pint (750 ml) milk
1 teaspoon (1 x 5 ml spoon) salt
cayenne pepper
1 medium onion, sliced
2 oz (50 g) hazlenuts, finely chopped

First make the béchamel sauce by melting the butter in a saucepan and mixing in the flour. Add the milk slowly to form a smooth sauce. Put in the onion and seasonings. Stir and cook gently for ten minutes.

To make the pancake batter, sift the flour and salt into a bowl and make a well in the middle. Crack the eggs into this and mix in the flour, a little at a time. Gradually add the milk and water together until you have a smooth batter.

Make your pancakes and set aside.

Cut your chosen vegetables into manageable pieces and stir-fry them in a little oil with the diced ginger, herbs, salt and pepper.

Stuff your pancakes with the vegetable mixture and roll up in a shallow ovenproof dish. Add the chopped nuts to the béchamel sauce and pour over the pancakes.

Put under a grill until the pancakes are heated through and the top is crisp and bubbling.

Cheese and Lovage Soufflé

Serves 4

This unusual soufflé comes from Diane Davies and is part of her "Summer Dinner at Downton". Diane writes, "Lovage is quite a strong herb, so experiment with the quantity of leaves you use. Most people I cook for like their soufflés very runny, so I usually only cook them for 20 minutes and make sure everyone is sitting down in plenty of time."

1½ oz (40 g) butter
2 tablespoons (2 x 15 ml spoons) flour
½ pint (300 ml) hot milk
4 eggs separated with 1 extra white
handful of lovage leaves, blanched and drained
4 oz (100 g) grated Cheddar cheese
salt, pepper, nutmeg

Melt the butter, add the flour and cook for one minute without browning. Remove from heat and beat in milk and cook for a further couple of minutes. Beat in the puréed lovage leaves, and egg yolks separately or put the whole thing into a magimix and add the egg yolks one by one with the machine running. (It can be prepared ahead of time to this stage.) Beat the egg whites

59

until stiff and carefully fold the two mixtures together. Turn into a buttered soufflé dish; the mixture should not come more than ⅔ way up the dish.

Preheat oven to 400°, Gas Mark 6 and bake until well risen and golden brown on top.

Spring Cabbage Fricassée with Cauliflower and Hazel Nut Salad

Serves 4

This recipe comes from Stafford Whiteaker, author of *The Compleat Strawberry*, a lovely book which has everything you could possibly want to know about strawberries.

Meanwhile, this fricassée is a favourite of his and he writes, "The moment winter air begins to warm and morning arrives with sunlight, I make up my mind that spring is here. Recipes for stews and hearty food are forgotten and the first meal of spring greens is full of the promise of vegetables and fruits to come."

Spring greens are a much maligned vegetable. Cooked properly, they have a superb taste. It is important to cut them into ribbons, rather than just tearing them.

2 oz (50 g) honey-baked ham (boiled ham will do as a second best)
2 large heads spring greens
1 teaspoon (1 x 5 ml spoon) whole mustard
4 big drops wine vinegar
pinch of sugar
1 medium onion, diced
⅔ clove garlic, diced not crushed
1 tablespoon (1 x 15 ml) spoon olive oil
water
rice

For the salad:
1 small cauliflower
2 tablespoons (2 x 15 ml spoons) hazelnut oil
2 tablespoons (2 x 15 ml spoons) roasted whole hazelnuts
salt and freshly ground black pepper

Wash and chop the spring greens into ribbons. Put them to one side and leave wet. Heat the olive oil in a saucepan and gently cook the diced onion. Cut the ham in little pieces and add to the onion with the garlic, mustard, vinegar and sugar.

Simmer for ten minutes then add the spring greens and half a cup of water. Cook rapidly for 15 - 20 minutes until the greens have become dark and wilted. Do not let them dry out and add more water if necessary.

At this point make the salad by breaking the cauliflower into tiny florets. Plunge these in boiling salted water and boil for 3 minutes. Strain through a colander and rinse in cold water to stop the cooking process. Drain and pat dry.

In a small bowl mix the hazel nut oil with some salt and pepper and the hazel nuts. Add the florets and toss until they are coated. The salad should be warm, crunchy, and highly aromatic.

Serve the spring greens surrounded by a circle of white rice and accompanied by the cauliflower and hazelnut salad.

Butter Bean, Leek, Tofu, and Mushroom Pie

Serves 6

This delicious, creamy pie comes from Carrie Eide who teaches vegetarian and vegan cooking from her home in South Shropshire. Vegan cooking allows no animal products hence the use of soya milk in the recipe. However, cows' milk can be used just as well, if preferred.

Tofu is soya bean curd and high in protein. On its own, it tastes of very little but absorbs the flavours it is cooked with and gives a wonderful creaminess to the pie.

8 oz (225 g) butter beans
3 leeks
1 onion
4 oz (100 g) mushrooms
2 cloves garlic
¾ pint (450 ml) soya or cows' milk
2 oz (50 g) margarine
2 tablespoons (2 x 15 ml spoons) flour
2 teaspoons (2 x 5 ml spoons) wet mustard
2 teaspoons (2 x 5 ml spoons) tamari
good bunch chopped parsley or coriander leaves
good pinch cayenne pepper
salt and pepper
tofu
4 oz (100 g) pastry

Soak and simmer the butter beans until they are soft. Chop and fry the onion and garlic in margarine for five minutes, and add mushrooms. Cook until soft, then stir in the flour and add the milk. Cook for a few minutes to make a thick white sauce. Add the mustard, tamari, parsley or coriander, cayenne, salt and pepper to taste. Stir well. Add the leeks, washed and cut into rounds. Cook for five minutes and pour into pie dish. Cut up some tofu and gently stir in.

Roll out the pastry to make a lid. Put in an oven preheated to 400°, Gas Mark 6 and bake in the centre for 20 minutes. Then turn down to 350°, Gas Mark 5, and cook for a further 15 - 20 minutes.

Serve with a crisp green salad.

Stuffed Pancakes with Wem-style Beetroot and Leek Mash

Serves 6

For this last recipe I thought I would mix the old and the new. The stuffed pancakes come from Carrie Eide and the beetroot and leek mash is an old recipe from Woodhouse Hall in West Felton. The two go very well together.

Pancake batter made from whole wheat flour, salt and water
8 oz (225 g) kidney beans
8 oz (225 g) mushrooms
1 large onion
2 cloves garlic
1 tin of tomatoes, drained
1 tablespoon (1 x 15 ml spoon) oil
chopped parsley
good bunch fresh basil or thyme, chopped
or 1 dessertspoon (1 x 10 ml spoon) dried basil or thyme
salt and pepper
margarine
grated cheese (optional)

Soak and cook the kidney beans. Chop the onion and the garlic and fry in the oil until clear. Add the tomatoes, and season with salt and pepper. Cook vigourously until fairly thick, then add the mushrooms and cook for a few more minutes. Add the beans and the chopped herbs. Check for seasoning and add the chopped parsley.

Stuff enough pancakes for six people and arrange in a shallow dish. Cover with grated cheese if desired and dot with margarine. Put in an oven preheated to 375°, Gas Mark 5, and cook until heated through.

To make the beetroot and leek mash, cook a couple of beetroots until they are soft. Peel and set aside. Finely chop a few leeks and fry in margarine or butter until they are soft.

Add the beetroot chopped into pieces and some milk. Cook together for a few minutes. Season with salt, pepper and a little lemon juice and mash together with a little more margarine if necessary.

Puddings

Soufflé Pancakes

Serves 6

A very simple and delicious pudding which can also be flavoured with vanilla, orange or lemon. Serve with thin butter biscuits (see recipe for Elderberry Ice Cream).

> *6 eggs, separated*
> *1 tablespoon (1 x 15 ml spoon) grated lemon rind*
> *¼ pint (150 ml) whipping cream*
> *Icing sugar to dredge*

Grease a skillet or an omelette pan with a little butter. Beat the yolks well and add to the cream. Then sprinkle in the lemon rind. Whip the whites until they are stiff and fold in the yolk mixture.

Fry in rounds like pancakes and dredge with icing sugar between each.

Darsham Pudding

Serves 6

There are many recipes for almond puddings. Some are baked on their own and others become the fillings for pies. This recipe, found in the Shrewsbury Records Office, calls for a mixture of wine or lemon juice, melted butter and sugar to be poured over the top while the pie is still warm.

3 oz (75 g) pudding rice
2 oz (50 g) ground almonds
2 eggs
2 tablespoons (2 x 15 ml spoon) sugar
lemon rind
vanilla
1/2 pint (300 ml)milk
8 oz (225 g) puff pastry
almond slivers

Wine or Lemon Sauce:
4 tablespoons (4 x 15 ml spoons) wine reduced by half
or 2 tablespoons (2 x 15 ml spoons) lemon juice
1 oz (25 g) butter
2 tablespoons (2 x 15 ml spoons) sugar

Boil the rice in creamy milk until it is soft. Strain and mix it with the ground almonds and sugar until it is smooth. Alternatively, put the whole lot in a magimix. Add the eggs, one at a time, and beat well.

Line an 8-inch pie dish with thin puff pastry. Spoon in the mixture and sprinkle with almond slivers. Bake in a hot oven, 425°, Gas Mark 7, for 15 minutes.

Mix the wine or lemon juice, sugar and butter in a saucepan and boil until the sugar has dissolved. Cook for a couple of minutes longer. Prick holes in the pie with a fork and pour the mixture over the top. Allow to cool slightly and serve with cream.

Mytton Pudding

Serves 6

Squire John Mytton, of Halston, Shropshire, was born in 1796 and later became MP for Shrewsbury and High Sheriff for the county. He was notorious for his "eccentric and extravagant exploits", and his biographer notes that "There was about him that which resembles the restlessness of the hyena".

He is perhaps best known for riding a bear into his drawing-room while dressed in full hunting costume.

However, the "proud Salopians" of his time disapproved of his bizarre behaviour and his political career was soon over.

The pudding is rich and looks most enticing.

1 plain sponge cake:
4 oz (100 g) self-raising flour
4 oz (100 g) butter or margarine
4 oz (100 g) sugar
2 eggs

For the pudding:
4 egg yolks
2 egg whites
2 glasses sherry or brandy
½ pint (300 ml) single cream
sugar
nutmeg
grated lemon peel
muscat raisins
flaked almonds
butter

Make your sponge cake the day before.

Grease a 3 pint (1½ litre) mould with butter. Press large muscat raisins against the sides, then line with a sponge cake cut into thin slices. Break pieces to make a good, tight fit. Carefully pour brandy or sherry over the cake lining. Fit the flaked almonds into the soaked cake.

Make a custard by heating the cream to boiling point. Meanwhile beat the egg yolks and sugar until they are light and creamy. Add the nutmeg and lemon peel. Whisk the whites until they are frothy. Pour the boiling cream over yolk and sugar mixture and beat well, then mix in the beaten whites.

Pour the whole thing into the cake mould and cook in a pan of hot water in the oven at 325°, Gas Mark 3, for 45 minutes. Allow to cool.

Cut away the brown edges of the cake slices so they are on the same level as the custard. Carefully immerse the mould in hot water for a minute or so until it is just warm enough to allow the pudding to slide out.

Wine Jelly

Serves 6

Wine jelly was a popular pudding in the 18th and 19th centuries. This modern recipe comes fom Diane Davies, and is especially good after a large, rich meal.

> *1 wetted jelly mould or 6 champagne flutes*
> *½ pint (300 ml) dry sherry*
> *4 tablespoons (4 x 15 ml spoon) orange juice*
> *3 tablespoons (3 x 15 ml spoon) lemon juice*
> *6 oz (150 g) sugar dissolved in ¾ pint (450 ml) boiling water*
> *gelatine*

Measure the liquid, including the sugar, and place in a bowl. For every pint of liquid dissolve ½ oz (15 g) or 1 sachet of gelatine in 2 tablespoons (2 x 15 ml spoon) of water in a saucepan. Do not boil. Stir into the rest of the liquid and put into a mould or glasses and allow to set.

Decorate with little sprigs of variegated lemon balm.

Silk Chiffon Pie

Serves 6

This is a very easy pudding from Pauline Napper and bears a strong resemblance to a speciality on which hung the reputation of Anatole, the culinary genius invented by Shropshire's P. G. Wodehouse.

Apart from the pre-baked pastry shell, there is no cooking to do. It is, however, most important to cream the butter and sugar really well, so that the sugar is completely dissolved. Castor sugar must be used.

> *1 pre-baked pastry shell*
> *4 oz (100 g) butter*
> *6 oz (150 g) caster sugar*
> *2 oz (50 g) good dark chocolate*
> *1 teaspoonful (1 x 5 ml spoon) vanilla essence*
> *2 eggs*
> *unsweetened whipped cream*
> *grated chocolate*

Cream the butter and sugar until the sugar has dissolved completely. Blend in the chocolate that has been melted and allowed to cool and add the vanilla essence. Beat in the eggs one at a time. Pour this smooth mixture into the pastry shell and chill for two hours.

Top with the whipped cream and sprinkle with grated chocolate.

Baked Apple Pudding

Serves 6

It was an old Shropshire belief that apples held powers of regeneration, and people thought it was lucky to burn apple logs to ward off evil influences.

This is another recipe from Rachel Leighton's book. It is a firm apple sauce pie filling, enlivened with a handful of chopped walnuts. It can be eaten warm or cold with lots of thick cream or whipped full cream yoghurt.

5 large cooking apples
5 oz (125 g) light brown sugar
2 oz (50 g) butter
3 eggs
juice and rind of one lemon
chopped walnuts (optional)
1 11-inch flan dish lined with pastry

Core, peel and chop the apples. Put them in a saucepan with the juice of a lemon. Simmer slowly until tender. Add the butter and sugar to taste. Stir the mixture until it is a smooth pulp and quite cool. When it is cold beat in the eggs, one by one. Then stir in the chopped nuts if used.

Line a flan dish with pastry and pour in the apple mixture. Sprinkle the top with brown sugar and bake in a moderate oven, 375°, Gas Mark 5, for 35 - 40 minutes. Allow the pie to cool slightly before serving or serve cold.

Pears with Strawberry Purée

Serves 6

This delicious fruit salad is the brainchild of Stafford Whiteaker, author of *The Compleat Strawberry*.

6 ripe pears
a little water flavoured with vanilla sugar
1 pint (600 ml) strawberry purée
sugar
kirsch
maraschino cherry juice

Peel the pears and poach in the flavoured water. Leave to cool in this syrup. Strain well, and arrange in a serving dish. Add sugar to the strawberry purée and mix in the kirsch and maraschino juice. Pour over the pears and serve.

Elderberry Ice Cream with Thin Butter Biscuits

Serves 8

Every September, Diane Davies travels north to the river Brora in Sutherland to cook for a party of fishermen. Just before she leaves, she picks the elderberries in her garden, and for their first supper she always gives them Elderberry Ice Cream.

The biscuits are easy to make, but watch them carefully, as they burn very quickly. Best made and eaten on the same day.

> *1 lb (450 g) elderberries*
> *6 oz (150 g) castor sugar*
> *½ pint (300 ml) whipped cream*
> *3 oz (75 g) icing sugar*
> *2 beaten egg whites*

Cook the elderberries until soft and rub through a sieve. Mix with the castor sugar and stir in the whipped cream. Add the icing sugar. Mix well and freeze until slushy. Fold in the beaten egg whites and freeze again.

To make the biscuits mix together 8 oz (225 g) self-raising flour with 6 oz (150 g) butter, 1 oz (25 g) icing sugar and a little vanilla essence. Put the mixture into a magimix or mix by hand. Roll out thinly, sprinkle with sugar and cut into rounds. Bake at 400°, Gas Mark 6, for 3 - 5 minutes.

A Pear Pye

Serves 6

This recipe comes from Rachel Leighton's cookbook. The pears are baked very slowly in red wine, or a mixture of cider and red wine, then baked again in a pie crust.

The final addition of a light custard mixture is well worth the extra time. It can be eaten hot or cold.

1½ lbs (775 g) cooking pears
red wine
5 oz (125 g) sugar
cloves
sweet pastry
sugar

For the custard:
¼ pint (100 ml) cream
2 egg yolks
brown sugar

Peel the pears, leaving the stalks on and keeping the peelings. Put them in a tall dish. Melt the sugar in enough wine to half cover the pears. Fill up to the top with water. Put in the peelings and bake on the lowest oven temperature for about 5 hours. When they are cooked and a dark brown colour, remove and allow to cool.

Make a sweet pastry and line an 11 inch pie dish. Carefully remove the pears and cut in half, taking out the pips. Put some of the cooking liquid in a saucepan and reduce slightly. Arrange the pears in the pie dish, pour over a little of the reduced wine and sprinkle with sugar. Bake in a moderate oven, 350°, Gas Mark 5, for 40 minutes or so.

About 5 minutes before the end of cooking time, mix up the egg yolks and cream and pour it over the top. Sprinkle with a little brown sugar and bake until just set.

Little Orange Custard Pots

Serves 6

These delectable little puddings come from The Old Post Office at Clun. They can be eaten hot or cold and if you really feel like spoiling yourself, instead of sprinkling sugar on the top, make an orange/Cointreau syrup, or for a sharper taste, an orange/Calvados syrup; turn out the custards and pour the syrup over the top.

6 egg yolks
3 egg whites
5 tablespoons (5 x 15 ml spoons) caster sugar
pinch of salt
vanilla pod
1¼ pints (750 ml) milk
grated rind and juice of 1 orange
2 tablespoons (2 x 15 ml spoons) Cointreau
unsalted butter

Beat the egg yolks and whites together with two tablespoons of the sugar and the pinch of salt. Heat the milk, freshly grated orange rind, vanilla pod and the rest of the sugar without letting it boil. Remove the vanilla pod. Pour the milk mixture over the egs, whisking all the time. Whisk in the orange juice and the Cointreau. Strain the mixture into well-buttered ramekins.

Place the ramekins in a pan of hot water and bake at 375°, Gas Mark 5, for about one hour until the custards are set. Sprinkle the top with raw cane sugar while still warm.

Hazelnut Meringues with Raspberry Purée

Serves 6

Another wonderful pudding from The Old Post Office. This is a good way to use fresh raspberries or, if you have some in the freezer, make a purée with them, as a taste of summer in the middle of a dark, wet winter.

For the meringues:
2 oz (50 g) hazelnuts,
4 egg whites
8 oz (225 g) castor sugar

For the purée:
8 oz (225 g) raspberries
1 oz (25 g) sugar

½ pint (300 ml) whipping cream

Put the shelled hazelnuts on an oven tray and roast in a hot oven, 400°, Gas Mark 6, for about 10 minutes. Shake tray from time to time to roast evenly. Remove when the skins have cracked and the nuts are a light golden colour. When they are cool, rub between your hands to remove the skins. Chop or crush very small in a coffee grinder or liquidizer. Run the machine in short bursts or the nuts will become buttery.

Mix the sugar with the ground nuts. To make the purée, sprinkle the sugar over the berries and leave for an hour for the juices to run. Liquidise and then sieve to remove the pips. If necessary, thin the purée with a little sweet white wine, as it should be slightly runny.

Whisk the egg whites at room temperatures in a clean bowl. Gradually add the sugar once the whites have begun to froth up. Beat constantly until all the sugar is use and the whites form stiff peaks. Carefully fold the hazelnut/sugar mixture into the meringue mix so that the nuts are evenly distributed. Spoon the meringue mix onto greased tinfoil on oven trays in two large rounds. Place on the lowest shelf in the oven and bake at 225°, Gas Mark 1 for at least two hours. If the centres are still soft, raise the temperature slightly, to dry them out.

Remove from oven and allow to cool.

Whip the cream until stiff. Spoon half of the cream onto one of the meringues and carefully put half the purée on top. Cover with the second meringue. Spoon over the rest of the cream and pour the remaining purée over the top.

Chocolate Drift

Serves 6

This recipe came from the 1970 edition of the W.I. cookbook called *A Cook For All Seasons*. It is easily made and can be decorated with whipped cream and nuts to make a rich and spectacular pudding.

> *4 oz (125 g) plain chocolate*
> *grated rind of 1 orange*
> *¼ pint (150 ml) double cream*
> *4 eggs, separated*
> *1½ oz (40 g) caster sugar*
> *whipped cream (optional)*
> *chopped nuts (optional)*

Melt the chocolate in a bowl over hot water. Remove from heat and beat in the egg yolks, orange rind and sugar, and allow to cool. Whip the cream util thick and stir into the chocolate mixture. Whip egg whites stiffly and fold into the chocolate mixture.

Pour into 1 large bowl or 6 little ones and chill. Decorate with whipped cream and nuts if liked.

Cakes

Shropshire Mint Cake

Mint cakes and Fig cakes were traditionally great favourites at village wakes and festivals. Fig cakes are made by substituting finely diced dried figs for the mint and currant filling given below, and were a specialtiy of Norton.

The earliest reference I could find to mint cakes was in an essay called *Seeds of Greediness*, published in 1825 by a Mrs. Cameron in which she states that "mint cakes among other things are . . . very tempting to children." And so they are. When I made them, the cakes were barely cold before they disappeared into a tangle of outstretched hands.

> *8 oz (225 g) shortcrust pastry and 1 dessertspoon caster sugar*
> *2 oz (50 g) butter*
> *2 tablespoons (2 x 15 ml spoons) finely chopped mint*
> *3 oz (75 g) currants*
> *3 oz (75 g) caster sugar*
> *beaten white of an egg*

Make the pastry, including the extra spoon of sugar. Sprinkle the chopped mint with half the specified sugar and leave for the juices to run. Then mix well with the butter, currants and the rest of the sugar.

Divide the pastry in two and roll out thinly into two squares the same size. Place one on a lightly greased baking sheet. Spread out the currant mixture and wet the edges of the pastry. Cover with the second square and press down the edges, sealing them together with the prongs of a fork.

Brush over with beaten egg white and sprinkle with caster sugar. Bake in a hot oven, 400°, Gas Mark 6, until golden brown. Allow to cool and cut into squares.

Market Drayton Gingerbread

The story behind this gingerbread reads like a detective thriller. The ginger, from Cochin in southern India, was brought back by Lord Clive, himself from Market Drayton.The gingerbread is made solely by the local firm of Billingtons, who keep the recipe secret to this day.

For the full story, read *Under the Buttercross* by Meg Pybus of Market Drayton, who gave me the recipe below. Not the secret one, of course, but quite delicious, nevertheless.

8 oz (225 g) plain flour
3 oz (75 g) butter
2 oz (50 g) golden syrup
4 oz (100 g) Demerara sugar
1 teaspoon (1 x 5 ml spoon) ginger
pinch of ground cloves and mace
½ egg
2 teaspoons (2 x 5 ml spoons) brandy

Melt syrup, butter and sugar in a saucepan. Stir in the flour, spices, egg and brandy. Let it stand in a cool place or a fridge for about 4 hours before rolling and cutting into biscuits or gingerbread men.

Bake on a greased tray at 350°, Gas Mark 5, for 25 minutes.

Shortbread

This recipe comes from the 1933 edition of the W.I. cookbook. Homemade shortbread is much better than what is produced commercially and it is easy to make.

Almond shortbread is made by adding 1 oz (25 g) ground almonds with 1 oz less rice flour and 1 oz less butter.

> *6 oz (150 g) butter*
> *6 oz (150 g) flour*
> *4 oz (100 g) caster sugar*
> *4 oz (100 g) castor sugar*
> *3 oz (75 g) rice flour*

Cream the butter and sugar and add the flour and rice flour. Mix all by kneading well together. Put the mixture in a shallow cake tin and press down with the flat of a knife. Sprinkle with sugar and cut into slices.

Bake in a moderate oven, 350°, Gas Mark 4, for 20 - 30 minutes. Allow to cool in the tin.

Shrewsbury Cakes or Biscuits

Shrewsbury was once famous for its cakes, which are now no longer made. The story of these cakes was published in 1938 in a pamphlet called, "Shrewsbury Cakes—The Story of a Famous Delicacy". We are told that the first mention of these cakes is in 1561 and that they were presented to distinguished personages on their visits to the town.

They had a chequered history, their baking being prohibited towards the end of the 16th century, for some mysterious reason. Luckily the bailiffs soon changed their minds and the cakes came back into favour. Indeed, in Cassell's *Dictionary of Cooking* printed in the 19th century, there are some five different methods listed for Shrewsbury Cakes.

8 oz (225 g) flour
4 oz (100 g) butter
4 oz (100 g) caster sugar
1 egg
2 teaspoons (2 x 5 ml spoons) grated lemon rind
pinch each, nutmeg, cinnamon, cloves

Cream the butter and sugar together and add the beaten egg a little at a time. Beat well. Add the sieved flour, lemon rind and spices and mix to a stiff paste. Turn out onto a floured board.

Knead lightly and roll out thinly. Cut into rounds, sprinkle with sugar and bake in a moderate oven, 350°, Gas Mark 4, for about 15 minutes. Allow to cool on a wire tray.

Soule Cakes

The recipe for these cakes comes from the Ward family of Pulverbatch and was given to Charlotte Burne, who wrote the definitive book on Shropshire Folklore at the end of the nineteenth century.

Mrs. Mary Ward was the last person to uphold the custom of giving out these cakes on All Saints Day. She lived to 101 and on her 100th birthday she dressed herself in her yellow satin wedding dress and received Holy Communion.

History has it that she never had an illness in all her long life.

3 lbs (1.5 kg) flour
8 oz (225 g) butter
8 oz (225 g) sugar
2 teaspoons (2 x 5 ml spoons) yeast
2 eggs
allspice
milk

Combine all ingredients except sugar and spice and leave to rise in a warm place. Mix in sugar and spice. Shape in flat buns, sprinkle with sugar and bake in a moderate oven, 350°, Gas Mark 4, until golden brown and cooked.

Simnel Cake

It was an old custom in Shropshire and especially in Shrewsbury to make these rich fruit cakes to give as presents at Easter and Mothering Sunday. The cake was encased in a stiff flour and water paste, coloured with saffron, first boiled, then brushed with egg and baked.

When it was eventually ready, the crust was apparently as hard as wood which was rather confusing to the lucky recipients. The story goes that one old lady used hers as a footstool for many years.

The recipe below comes from a 1914 cookbook book I found at the Radbrook Culinary Museum. It was prefaced by this poem:

She who would a Simnel make,
Flour and saffron first must shake,
Candy, spices, eggs must take,
Chop and pound till arms do ache.
Then must boil and then must bake,
For a crust too hard to break,
When at Mid-Lent she doth wake,
To her mother bear her cake,
Who will prize it for her sake.

The simnel cake here is baked in the usual way and then decorated with little almond balls.

1 lb (450 g) flour
8 oz (225 g) castor sugar
8 oz (225 g) butter
4 eggs
4 oz (100 g) candied lemon peel, chopped
¾ lb (350 g) sultanas
¾ lb (350 g) currants
1 teaspoon (1 x 5 ml spoon) cinnamon and ginger and nutmeg
1 teaspoon (1 x 5 ml spoon) baking powder
grated rind and juice of 1 orange and 1 lemon

4 oz (100 g) ground almonds
1 teaspoon (1 x 5 ml spoon) pure vanilla essence
few drops almond essence
1 teacup brandy or sweet sherry

For the almond balls:
8 oz (225 g) ground almonds
4 oz (100 g) icing sugar
4 oz (100 g) castor sugar
1 tablespoon (1 x 15 ml spoon) brandy or sherry
1 egg yolk
icing sugar to dust

The day before baking the cake put the sultanas, currants, chopped peel orange and lemon rind and juice and the sherry into a bowl and leave overnight.

Line an 8- or 9-inch cake tin with three layers of greaseproof paper. Cream the butter and sugar until light and fluffy. Beat in the eggs one by one and add the essences. Sift together the flour, baking powder, and spices.

Mix the flour and the fruit mixture alternately into the butter mixture, a little at a time. Finally stir in the ground almonds

Bake for 2 hours at 300°, Gas Mark 3, then turn down to 275°, Gas Mark 1, for a further 1½ hours. Leave cake to cool in its tin.

Wrap it in fresh greaseproof paper and leave to settle for a week. When you are ready to ice it, mix together the almonds and sugar and the brandy and slowly beat in the egg yolk. Shape into smooth little balls and roll in icing sugar. Decorate the cake with these and dredge with icing sugar.

Steamed Walnut Cake

This recipe comes from a Radbrook College class book, dated 1904. It was called a pudding, but actually makes a better cake when it is left to cool. It looks like a bit like a martian spaceship, being dome-shaped and studded with cherries.

4 oz (100 g) broken walnuts
3 eggs
3 oz (75 g) castor sugar
2 oz (50 g) flour
3 oz (75 g) butter
2 oz (50 g) rice flour
2 tablespoons (2 x 15 ml spoons) milk
1 teaspoon (1 x 5 ml spoon) vanilla
1 dessertspoon (1 x 10 ml spoon) grated plain chocolate
good pinch baking powder
glacé cherries

Butter a 2 pint bowl. Cream the butter and sugar and add the eggs one by one. Add the sifted flours and baking powder alternately with the milk. Stir in the nuts, grated chocolate and the vanilla essence.

Press the cherries onto the sides of the bowl and carefully spoon in the mixture. Take a piece of foil and make a pleat in the middle and cover the bowl. Tie it tightly around the edge. Stand the bowl on a metal trivet or ring in a saucepan and fill ⅔ with boiling water. Steam for 1½ hours. Carefully invert onto a plate and allow to cool. When serving, cut in thin slices because it is rather rich.

Apple Cake with Lemon Sauce

Children love this recipe, which comes from Christine Tait, who specializes in making delicious cakes. The apple slices are pushed down vertically so that they cook with the cake and stay moist, giving the cake a delicate apple flavour.

If you are eating the cake hot, make a sharp lemony sauce to go with it.

4 oz (100 g) self-raising flour
4 oz (100 g) butter or margarine
4 oz (100 g) sugar
2 eggs
pinch of allspice
brown sugar
cinnamon
2 large Bramley apples, peeled, quartered and thinly sliced

For the lemon sauce:
2 lemons
1½ pints (900 ml) water including lemon juice and grated rind
3 tablespoons (3 x 15 ml spoons) cornflour
3 tablespoons (3 x 15 ml spoons) sugar
added lemon juice and sugar to taste
knob of butter

Make a sponge by creaming the butter and sugar until light and fluffy, then add the eggs, one by one. Sift the flour with the spices and mix in with the butter mixture.

Pour the mixture into a cake tin with a removable base. Push the apples slices into the mixture in a circular pattern and sprinkle the top with brown sugar and cinnamon. Bake in a moderate oven 350°, Gas Mark 4, for about 40 minutes until done.

To make the lemon sauce, mix the cornflour with a little cold water and blend to a smooth paste with the sugar. Heat the lemon water to boiling and slowly add it to the cornflour paste, stirring all the time, until it is thick. Add a little butter and mix well and reheat if necessary.

Serve the cake hot with plenty of lemon sauce poured over the top.

Drinks, Pickles and Preserves

Button Onion Sauce

This recipe comes from Diane Davies. It is delicious with lamb or pork and could be used as a filling for a savoury flan.

2 lbs (almost a kilo) button onions
¼ pint (150 ml) chicken stock
dash of white wine or cider
2 oz (50 g) butter
2 tablespoons (2 x 15ml spoons) flour
¾ pint (450 ml) milk
¼ pint (150 ml) cream
salt and pepper
freshly grated nutmeg
lots of chopped parsley

Boil onions for a few minutes, then slip off the skins. Put into a clean pan with stock and wine or cider and simmer for 30 minutes. Make a sauce with butter, flour and milk and simmer for five minutes. Stir in cream, season with salt, pepper and nutmeg and add parsley. Drain the onions and add to the sauce. Check seasoning and serve very hot.

Yellow Pickle or Piccalilli

This recipe comes from a cookbook written in 1847 and deposited in the Shrewsbury Rcords Office by Lord Orlando Bridgman, a former Lord Lieutenant of Shropshire.

It is very much an individual pickle as it depends on what is in the vegetable garden when you make it or what is in season. Suitable vegetables are broccoli, kidney beans, small marrows, shallots, cucumbers, green cabbage, cauliflower, beans, celery and green tomatoes.

For every 4 lbs (2 kg) vegetables:
2½ standard bottles cider or wine vinegar
chillies, cloves, peppercorns

For the Yellow Dressing:
4 oz (100 g) flour, sieved
8 oz (225 g) sugar
4 oz (100 g) dry mustard
1 dessertspoon (1 x 10 ml spoon) turmeric
2 teaspoons (2 x 5 ml spoons) celery seed
scarce 1 teaspoon (1 x 5 ml spoon) ground allspice

brine:
4 oz (100 g) salt
2½ pints (1½ litres) water

Chop up the vegetables and soak them in brine for 24 hours. Bring to the boil, strain, and leave a little while to dry. Tie the chillies, cloves and peppercorns in a muslin bag and bruise. Boil gently for 45 minutes and strain.

In a heavy pan, combine all the dressing ingredients including the vinegar and stir over a medium heat until you have a thick, smooth sauce. Add the vegetables to this sauce and stir to heat through and coat them.

Pot in vinegar-proof jars while still hot. Seal and keep for at least three months before using.

Damson Chutney

People with damson trees in their gardens are always looking for ways to use up the fruit. This dark red chutney keeps well and makes a very popular present especially for friends living in the city.

I often use chutneys in stews and pot roasts for a change in taste. This recipe makes six 1lb jars.

4 lbs (almost 2 kg) damson plums, washed and stoned
1½ lbs (475 g) cooking apples, peeled and chopped
3 cloves garlic, crushed
3 dried chillies
1 lb (450 g) seedless raisins
2 pints (1 litre) cider vinegar
1 tablespoon (1 x 15 ml spoon) ground ginger
1 teaspoon (1 x 5 ml spoon) allspice
1 teaspoon (1 x 5 ml spoon) dried mustard
1 teaspoon (1 x 5 ml spoon) salt
1½ lb (675 g) light brown sugar

Put the apples, plums, raisins, chillies, garlic and vinegar into a saucepan. Bring to the boil and cook gently for 10 minutes. Add the sugar and stir constantly until the chutney thickens. After about 15 minutes add the rest of the spices and cook for a further 15 minutes.

Pot in sterilized jars while it is still hot.

Pickled Eggs

Homemade pickled eggs are delicious and quite different from the factory produced variety. This recipe comes from the 1933 W.I. cookbook.

8 fresh eggs
1 pint (600 ml) white wine vinegar
4 cloves
small piece bruised ginger
1 chilli
1 clove garlic
few peppercorns
1 teaspoon (1 x 5 ml) salt

Boil the eggs for 15 minutes. Put the other ingredients in a saucepan and simmer for 5 minutes. Shell the eggs and put them into a dry, wide-necked jar.

Pour the boiling vinegar over the eggs. Press down to get rid of any air bubbles and leave to get cold. Cover and seal.

To Pickle French Beans

This recipe comes from Rachel Leighton's cookbook. It is an excellent way of using up beans when they are in season and you have a surplus. They also make excellent presents; the green beans look rather pretty with the strips of red pepper and the chillies.

2 lbs (900 g) young French beans, trimmed
2 large red peppers, cut in strips
1 large Spanish onion, thinly sliced
3 dried red chillies
fresh tarragon or summer savory
1 tablespoon (1 x 15 ml spoon) salt
1 pint (600 ml) white wine vinegar

Lay the vegetables on a flat serving dish (not metal) and sprinkle liberally with salt. Leave overnight.

Put all the other ingredients, except the fresh herbs and chillies, into a saucepan and simmer gently for five minutes. Drain the beans and add to the vinegar. Boil for a couple of minutes until beans are cooked but still crunchy.

Lift out vegetables with a slotted spoon and pack into sterilized jars, putting a chilli and a few fresh herbs into each. Bring the vinegar back to the boil and fill jars to overflowing. Press down vegetables with a spoon to release any trapped air. Seal immediately.

Preserved cherries

I found this recipe scrawled on the back of a handbill of a performance for Hoffman's Organophobic Band at The Parochial School Room in Ironbridge in 1855. It was obviously a good show, as Mr. Hoffman states that, as a result of popular demand, "his Organophobic Band will give one more, but positively the last, Entertainment in this locality."

The cherries are good, too.

2lbs (900 g) ripe morello cherries
1½ lbs (6750 g) sugar
¾ pint (450 ml) sweet white wine
¼ pint (150 ml) brandy

Take the stalks out of the cherries and prick all over with a pin. Sprinkle half the sugar over the cherries and leave overnight. Dissolve the other half in the wine and brandy. Add the cherries and sugar and bring to the boil. Leave overnight again. Bring to boil the next day. Remove the cherries with a slotted spoon and put into jars. Boil the remaining syrup to reduce it slightly and pour over the cherries. Press down the contents to release any trapped air and seal.

Pickled Damsons

This is a traditional way of using up damsons. They go very well with cold meat and poultry.

> 6lbs (2.8 kg) damsons
> 6 lbs (2.8 kg) sugar
> 3 pints (1¾ litres) cider vinegar
> few cloves
> 1 cinnamon stick

Prick the fruit with a pin and put in a large basin. Boil the vinegar, sugar and spices tied in a bag and pour over the fruit. Leave overnight. Carefully strain off the liquid and bring to the boil again. Pour over the fruit and leave for one night again. Boil the liquid and fruit together for one minute.

Lift the fruit with slotted spoon and pack into jars. Reduce the liquid slightly and pour over the top. Release any trapped air and seal.

Pickled Pears

This is a good pickle to make in the autumn when pears are cheap and plentiful. Always use under-ripe pears.

> 6 lbs (2.8 kg) hard pears, peeled
> 2 lbs (900 g) sugar
> 1 pint (600 ml) cider vinegar
> 4 cloves
> 2 cinnamon sticks

Cut the pears in half and carefully remove the cores. Boil sugar, vinegar and spices together for 10 minutes. Remove the cinnamon sticks and add the pears. Simmer until just tender. Put the pears into jars and if necessary boil liquid until a syrup forms. Pour over the pears, and release any trapped air. Top up with syrup and seal.

Mint Sauce for Wintertime

This recipe comes from *A Cook for All Seasons*, the 1970 W.I. cookbook. Pick the mint on a dry day and chop it finely. You will need a good bundle.

> *1 pt (600 ml) wine or cider vinegar*
> *1 lb (450 g) sugar*
> *mint*

Boil the vinegar and sugar and leave to cool. Chop the mint and pack into jars. Pour over the cold vinegar and cover with vinegar-proof covers. This will keep for six to nine months until the next crop of fresh mint leaves appears.

Honey Mint Sauce

I thought this was a good idea from the same W.I. cookbook.

> *1 cupful finely chopped mint*
> *3 tablespoons (3 x 15 ml spoon) honey*

Combine mint and honey in the given proportions and store in screw-topped jars. Dilute with vinegar as and when required.

Damson Cheese

There is a delightful story in *Under the Buttercross* about the King of Nepal and his liking for Market Drayton Damson Cheese.

Apparently, during the King's last visit to London, he ordered his favourite meal of Roast Lamb and Damson Cheese for his Guildhall Banquet. (A few years before his wife had bought some at the Royal Show and he had a hankering for another taste of it.)

91

Accordingly, an order for 2 cwt of Damson Cheese was passed on to Market Drayton WI, to be delivered two days later . . . They rose gallantly to the challenge; helpers were marshalled and freezers raided and somehow 2 cwt of purple-black damson cheese was packed into jars and arrived at the Guildhall just in time for the banquet.

damsons
water
sugar

Put the clean fruit in a pan. Add water about half way to the top of the fruit. Simmer gently until fruit is thoroughly soft and pulpy. This will take time, as damson skins are tough and must be thoroughly softened. Rub the pulp and add 1 lb of sugar for every 1 lb of fruit. Boil for 1 - 1¼ hours, stirring constantly and taking care to scrape the bottom of the pan from time to time. Pack into clean jars and seal.

Orange and Lemon Squash

Homemade squash tastes so much better than the commercial varieties.

This recipe comes from Diane Davies.

4 oranges
2 lemons
2½ lbs (1.6 kg) sugar
1 oz Citric Acid (from any chemist)
3 pts (1½ litres) boiling water

Thinly pare the rinds from the fruit and put into a large bowl. Dissolve the citric acid in a small cup of boiling water, and add to the bowl with the sugar. Pour in the boiling water and stir well until all the sugar has dissolved. Squeeze the juice from the fruit and add it to the water.

Pour the cordial into bottles. Leave the rinds in; they sink to the bottom and help maintain the flavour.

Elderberry Syrup

Make this syrup when elderberries are ripe and keep it in the cupboard for winter colds and flu. It helps ward off colds and relieves chest troubles.

elderberries
sugar
water
12 cloves
1 teaspoon (1 x 5 ml spoon) ginger
1 teaspoon (1 x 5 ml spoon) cinnamon

Gather ripe berries and wash them. Put in a large saucepan and cover with water. Simmer well. To every pint of juice, add 1 lb sugar and spices. Boil again for at least 30 minutes to form a thick syrup. Bottle when cold.

Take 1 tablespoon (1 x 15 ml spoon) in boiling water at the onset of a cold.

Index